About the authors

Manjit Sargam Chawla is manager in a nationalized bank, but a motivational speaker, corporate trainer, author and a blogger by passion. She used to give free motivational classes for students and people in the corporate world, to help them live their life to the fullest. Ever since birth, she has been a devotee of Sant Nirankari Mission and learnt a lot from Satguru Baba Hardev Singh ji.

She has earlier written *The Mystic of Twin Flame Relationship* on reincarnation of souls and meeting of souls in earthy planes. She loves to serve humanity and is very spiritual. She strongly believes that positive attitude and subconscious mind can create miracles. The aim of her life is to spread smiles and happiness wherever she goes or through prayers where she can't go. Her dreams comprise love, humanity and spiritual awakening of each and every human being.

Yogi Amrit Raj is a fourth generation, award winning Ayurvedic Doctor and Certified 200/500 Hour Yoga Teacher from Yoga Alliance USA. Yogi Dr. Amrit Raj has given lectures, seminars and classes on Ayurveda and yoga in a number of renowned institutions. He is an honorary visiting professor in Dinacharya Ayurvedic Institute in New York.

Outside of India, he provides spiritual retreats and Yoga camps and offers spiritual and Ayurvedic lifestyle consultations at India's Arogyadham Center. He is a regular writer at Speakingtree. in. For the past five years, he has provided charitable services in yoga & Ayurveda both in India and abroad. He is also Trustee of Arogyadham Global AIDS Research Foundation and is the founder of Maa Yoga Ashram in Tapovan, Rishikesh. He has conducted Yoga and Ayurveda workshops/ sessions for former President of India Smt Pratibha Patil, royal families of Europe, United Nations, among others.

Live, Love and Laugh

Manjit Sargam Chawla

inspired by Yogi Amrit Raj

Srishti
Publishers & Distributors

Srishti Publishers & Distributors
Registered Office: N-16, C.R. Park
New Delhi – 110 019
Corporate Office: 212A, Peacock Lane
Shahpur Jat, New Delhi – 110 049
editorial@srishtipublishers.com

First published by
Srishti Publishers & Distributors in 2019

10 9 8 7 6 5 4 3 2 1

This is a work of non-fiction, based on the authors' experiences and life-learnings. It provides practical solutions to everyday problems, but the recommendations given herein are in no way intended to be a substitute for professional advice and help.

My heartfelt gratitude towards
my husband Rajeev Chawla,
my kids Shudhita and Pushpit,
who encourage me, motivate me and
set me free to spread my wings to fly high.
Lots of love...

The book is dedicated to all our readers.
We want you all to live a
happy, healthy and peaceful life.

Live, Love and Laugh is dedicated to all those
Who are struggling with their thoughts,
Are under anxiety and stress,
Who need a helping hand to improve their finances,
Who need true guidance to improve their relationships,
Who need a true guide to stay healthy,
Who need to grow, both internally and externally
Who need the key to the secret lock of the Universe's wisdom.

Contents

Acknowledgements

The completion of this book could not have been possible without the participation and assistance of so many people, whose names may not all be enumerated. Their contributions are sincerely appreciated and gratefully acknowledged.

My heartfelt gratitude towards Sristhi Publishers & Distributors, for trusting my work and helping in every possible way.

My heartfelt thanks towards all the relatives, friends and others who in one way or another shared their support, either morally, financially or physically. Thank you so much.

Above all, to the great king almighty formless, the author of all knowledge and wisdom, the key to all secrets of the universe, grateful for showing its kingdom to me and teaching me to live every moment, to love beyond words and to laugh every day.

Introduction

"You shall be able to do marvellous things when you start using the magical powers of your Subconscious Mind."

—Dr Joseph Murphy (1898-1981 AD)
The Power of Your Subconscious Min'

Every person in this universe wants happiness and peace of mind. The last wish of each and every person is only happiness, whether in the form of divine contentedness, health, wealth, mental happiness or peace at the level of the soul.

With the grace of the Formless Almighty, I am writing this book for a feeling of joy and to attain the inner peace with a good health to manifest each and every dream you see in your life.

The book will help you with the art of living. If you are wondering how yoga and the law of attraction come together, notice how it works. It will teach you to:

- All that you experience in your lives, you have attracted (both the good and the bad) by your thoughts, feelings, prayers, actions, inactions, decisions and soul's energy level.

- You can change your circumstances by changing the way you think (and feel), altering what you believe, what you say to yourselves (self-talk) and the actions you take.
- The energy needed to make your dreams come true is already around you, it's already available in your mind and heart. It is waiting for your thoughts and beliefs to manifest it into the material world.
- Love is the energy; belief is the vehicle for manifestation. There exists nothing which is stronger than love and belief.

If you need a good health, then here it is…

If you need riches, money and luxury, then here it is…

If you need love, respect and care in relationships, then here it is…

Yes! All the dreams are here.

Peace, respect, money, riches, travel, dream home, dream cruise, dream business.

All that you want…

Here it all is…

1

Art of Living: Basics of Manifestation

Thoughts and their Vibrational Frequency

"Thoughts are living things – they travel far."

–Swami Vivekananda

Due to some unknown fears of my subconscious mind, I woke up from my deep sleep. Waiting for sleep to greet me once again, logged into my social media account, only to see the picture of a Syrian child's dead body lying on the seashore. I was in deep grief and pain, worried about the innocent people who have been killed. I woke my husband up and insisted on him to pray for humanity with me, around 1:30 a.m. Moreover, to pray for so many countries that are suffering and bleeding at the mercy of terrorist attacks. After praying to the Almighty, my husband pampered me and somehow managed to make me sleep.

Early the next morning, I got a phone call from one of my friends, Mr Surjit Budhiraja, and he asked a question; "Why are you interfering in the will of God? Praying can be considered alright, but to act stubborn in front of the almighty is not at all good."

A chill went down my spine and I asked, "How do you know what happened? How do you know that I prayed the whole night for humanity and terrorism affected countries and was acting stubborn before almighty?"

I heard silence in response.

This is how the vibrational frequencies of a person can be easily felt by another person.

This is how the frequency of our thoughts makes our aura.

Have you ever wondered that 'thoughts' are also living beings?

Thoughts are like seeds that you plant in your mind and feed them, nurture them with your learning and perceptions. A positive attitude strengthens the plant and empowers the thoughts, and ultimately empowers life. However, if you let weeds grow its roots in your mind, then you won't be able to attain the pinnacle of mental peace and eternal happiness.

Whatever you think is sown on the land of your mind, and the result of the thought is what you cut as the ripe crop. Every thought is associated with a certain vibrational frequency and each thought carries its energy at a different frequency.

You are just a bunch of thoughts and impressions. Those thoughts, which are positive, uplifting and in harmony with the universe, love and joy have a faster frequency of consciousness and they contain more light energy. Everything is made up of vibrations and all vibrations are a part of one soul, that is 'The Super Soul'.

It is a method of describing the overall state of a person. Everything in the universe is made up of energy vibrating at different frequencies.

The soul, super soul and entire species of flora and fauna of the universe are a form of energy. As you know, energy can neither be created, nor can it be destroyed. Energy can only be transformed from one form to another.

Even objects are made up of vibrational energy fields, just like you and me. The only difference is that everyone's energy is vibrating at a different frequency and at a different level. A person's vibration is a way of describing his/her overall state of being.

From scientific and metaphysical perspectives, we are made up of different energy levels which are – physical, mental, emotional and spiritual. Each of these levels has vibrational frequencies, which combine to create an overall vibration of a being which we also call an 'aura' of a person.

Albert Einstein in 1905 discovered 'Ignited Humanity's Curiosity'. Einstein proved through quantum physics that energy and matter are interchangeable and interconnected. The formless universe (cosmos) and all things within it are interchangeable. Your energy, vibrational frequency and physical self-care are interchangeable.

You are a universal energy that is a soul manifesting itself in various forms throughout the universe and it comes from the super soul (the highest energy, the source).

The original substance is the vibrating energy from which all the living and non-living beings come out. The difference between an organism's energy and non-living things is that they are made up of different vibrational frequencies.

That way, the matters we deal with are like the imagination of the thoughts which occupy our mind, and ultimately, the mind of 'the source'. Imagination in thought-processing can easily be created by the power of positive thoughts. So precisely speaking, all living and non-livings things are a product of a thought.

It is thought from which all things are made and which in its original state, permeates, penetrates and fills the interspaces of the universe and hence gets manifested in the real form. The only thing that matters is the frequency of your vibrations.

There are two types of vibrational frequencies – the lower vibrations and the higher vibrations. Lower vibrations of a person are associated with disempowering thoughts like guilt, jealousy, lack of self-worth, negative emotions, poor health, and lack of spiritual awareness.

Higher vibrations, on the other hand, are associated with empowering thoughts, positive emotions, gratitude, appreciation, acceptance, good health and strong spiritual awareness.

> *"You emit an energy, which can easily be felt by people around you. The more positive and better you are, the happy your surroundings feel."*

We all were busy gossiping and eating food at a certain party; there was somehow a little sadness and negativity in the environment. Rajeev arrived at the party and suddenly we all felt happy. The environment of the party was transformed into joy and enjoyment. "His presence made things lively and positive," one of the guests stated.

But what had happened in the party after Rajeev came?

Rajeev had the positive high vibration frequency which made other people calm and joyous. It was the inner pleasant music in Rajeev's soul which was heard by the others and that paved the way for positivity and calmness.

Your thought system decides the height and depth of your vibrational frequencies. It is this system that tells you whether you are having high or low frequency. You become what you think. Your subconscious mind has some thoughts associated with your lives and that, without letting your conscious mind know, makes your destiny. Old belief system, and perceptions make your entire being. Positive and negative thoughts are distinguishable like noise and musical notes.

The sound you make with your thoughts will determine the outside world. You can create music into your mind through positive thoughts. You can attract miracles into your lives by changing your old perceptions and old belief systems by raising your overall vibrations. In other words by, making all your thoughts positive and empowering, you can bring about a major change in your life.

The price of greatness is a responsibility for each of your thoughts.

Now, to take this notion further, to attract the miracles and to fulfill one's dreams:

"Every positive musical note within you creates a song in the world surrounding you."

Attract Miracles through the Power of your Mind and Thoughts

> *"A thought in this essential substance produces what this thought imagines. An individual can imagine things in his or her mind, and if she prints this thought in the amorphous substance, he or she will be able to generate what the thought imagines."*
>
> –*The Science of Getting Rich* by Wallace Wattles

Like attracts like. Actually, you all are magnets because you are made up of energy which is vibrating constantly and attracts the same vibrations. So ultimately, what you are and what you want to be in your life attracts each other. Perception in your subconscious mind works for you and it always comes in front of you. It's the vibrational frequency in which you are. You attract the things, people and circumstances having the same frequencies.

The thoughts you have related to money, relationships, home, business or any subject, cause a vibrational environment that brings to you the people and circumstances that surround you. Everything that comes to you is about what you've got going on a specific vibration, and what you've got going on that specific vibration is usually because of what you are keenly observing. But it does not have to necessarily be like this.

A mind is like a mirror, always reflecting back to you what you see out there. So, the higher the frequency of your thoughts and your feelings, the more miraculous the outcome will be. Therefore, think whatever is of high vibrational frequency and you will get a higher frequency in return; just like the process of reflection.

One of my favourite poets is Jalal-ud-Din Muhammad Rumi, a twentieth-century Sufi philosopher and poet. He was an exceptional guide for personal and spiritual growth with extraordinary persuasive power. He said; *"That whatever you seek is seeking you. Whatever you want is really wanting you, you should just have that dedication and desire to achieve it."*

So whatever you think of, whatever you want through your conscious and subconscious minds, you attract the same into your lives.

I have seen many couples who are living happily from the past so many years. Although when they got married, they had different mindsets, different priorities and different thinking, but gradually when they came in the same vibrational frequencies, same perceptions and same thoughts, then their behaviour began to be similar. As if they were born for each other. How does that happen?

The only answer is; *"Like attracts like."*

If you are happy, you will attract happy people. If you are sad or upset, you will attract the same emotions and circumstances the whole day, whole week and whole life until you raise your frequency. Your risen frequency purifies your aura.

People usually complain, *"It was a very bad day!"* Why?

They become upset over petty and trivial things. For example, you go to brush your teeth in the morning and the toothpaste tube is empty. Is it a reason good enough for being upset or ruining your whole day?

One more example is, you got a phone call from your house maid that she won't be coming and you start yelling at yourself and your kids, not because they did something wrong, but because you are in anxiety and stress about the pending household chores. You did completed work in just an hour, but the stress you went through spoilt your whole day. Mostly it is seen that people tend to lower their vibrational energy and hence spoil their day.

As lower frequency attracts lower frequency, on such days, you will attract the kind of people who have lower frequency and thus you will attract negative circumstances into your life.

So, don't feel bad for the little and trivial things, don't lower your vibrations, go for higher frequency and you will feel fantastic.

Throughout your daily life, you interact with so many people. Every moment has an impact on your overall energy level and your state of being at that very moment. Every choice in the day influences you to move on a good energy level or a bad one. The choice is yours; either you go with higher frequency or stay with a lower one.

> *"When a thought or a wish makes you feel excited, then that thought should be sustained for a long period of time to manifest your dream."*

A person is literally what he thinks; the sum total of the thoughts of person makes his character. The character of a person is what a person thinks and makes a regular habit of it. Whatever you choose as your habit, ultimately becomes your character.

To increase my energy level, I chose kindness. In my job, I spread smiles. All the strangers who come in front of me are mostly grown-ups and tired of their lives. I try to make them smile and make them feel happy in the least possible time. I used to keep so many candies in my drawer, so that every time a child come, I would give him/her a candy. I'm sharing an incident with you.

An old man named Bali Ram Ji used to come weekly to the bank, just to understand the fixed deposit schemes. All the staff members including the branch head felt irritated whenever he came. As I tried to make everyone happy and comfortable in the bank, I offered him a cup of tea and something to eat and talked to him politely and lovingly. He was quite satisfied with me and from then onwards, he always wanted to meet me whenever he came to the bank.

One day, he offered me a share in his wealth. I was shocked and all the staff members, including me, started laughing loudly. I told him, if you want to give me anything, please give me your blessings.

Practicing kindness and smiling throughout the day, even to strangers and other people in your life will nourish your soul and always maintain your high vibrations.

So, judge yourself. Determine whether you are increasing your frequency or lowering it.

When you are overwhelmed with hatred, complaints, guilt, fear, sadness, anxiety, etc., you enter into a lower energy state, due to which, you block the good vibrations which arrive from spirituality and positivity. Lower energy state may bring depression, anxiety and many other physical and mental health challenges. So, you have to raise your vibrations to stay connected with the Almighty, with the universe or with the 'super soul'.

Low vibrations remind me of the old me. I was depressed because I was not having good relations with my husband and family. I was full of negative thoughts, had a deep fear and very low self-esteem. Meanwhile, I forgot to love myself too. That became the cause of deep anxiety, which ultimately led me to heart disease in my twenties.

Such low vibrational thoughts always destroy you.

By raising your vibrations, you can experience the true state of intuition, joy, happiness, satisfaction, love and connection with almighty.

The high vibrational frequency is one in which a person is enlightened with the formless almighty, the universe, the super soul and feels immense happiness. It's the state of contentment; increasing spiritual awareness can attract anything and anyone in life. Whether it's about success, money, health, happiness, dreams, or everything that you want in your life. Increase your vibrations by feeling good and happy and all your dreams will find their destination in your hands and pockets.

Dirty water can be done away with by constantly pouring pure water into it. In the same way negative thoughts can be changed by pouring positive thoughts on it again and again.

Whenever we go to seek blessings (for exams, interviews or anything else) of our beloved uncle Mr Avtar Singh ji in the Nirankari congregation, he replies instantly: "Blessings are all in your pockets. Just have faith; stay happy and whatever you seek will be yours."

Your subconscious perception makes you and your character. Whatever you have become is the product of your thought. If you will think positive, you will feel positive. When you are on a higher vibrational frequency, gradually the perception of your subconscious mind gets rooted deep inside you.

> *"You yourself are a creator of your destiny; choose your thoughts wisely."*

Self Love

> *"Accept everything about yourself. I mean everything. You are you, and that is the beginning and the end. No apologies, no regrets."*
>
> –Henry A Kissinger, American diplomat and political scientist *(September 22, 1973 – January 20, 1977)*

Practice self-love, happiness, and positivity as you are special and a unique child of this universe. The most powerful thing in the entire universe is love. However, it's not only the love that you give to others, but also the love you give to yourself – 'self love'. Relieve yourself from all senses of guilt, resentment, anger, jealousy, and try to be cool, calm, happy and excited.

I once again remind you that you are the unique and special child of this universe, that the almighty made you with your special traits, special behaviour, special smile, special beauty, special talent, special intelligence and much more. Love yourself as *you are*.

When I was suffering from deep guilt, anxiety and depression, my husband gifted me some self-help books to read, which made me aware of the vibrational frequencies and how it worked. I was on medication at that time and all the negative feelings wiped off all good feelings from my life. I closed my academy; I was not able to sleep for months. There was not a single sign of smile on my face. My family and my kids were disturbed. Nevertheless, after reading that book and due to sincere efforts of my husband, I was able to leave all anti-depressants in just four months.

Slowly I transformed myself and tried to think positive. Gradually it became a habit for me and led me towards a prosperous and happy life ahead.

Now nothing can stop me from being happy and laughing.

You are the child of the almighty and you are the most precious to him. Spreading love, kindness, compassion and forgiveness can heal you from inside out. Be kind to yourself and tell yourself how beautiful you are. You are a winner and you can make amazing decisions. You deserve abundance. You may fail or lose at times, but you will never lose lessons and experiences from failure.

Acceptance is the only thing which makes a person fly high in the sky. Acceptance is not about denying our histories, but being wholly in the present moment and surrendering to whatever is happening. That is not to say that you give in or give up hoping for the better. Surrender just means saying yes to now. The past is unchangeable and the future is yet to come, so 'now' is all we really have.

So, now onwards, accept everything about yourself. You are beautiful as you are. Whatever you had in your past is just a lesson and an experience, nothing more than that. Lack of self-acceptance attracts all sorts of negative thoughts that feed on positivity and you don't want that to happen in order to live peacefully. Doing lovely things to yourself will enhance self-love and that will help you to accept yourself truly. Treat yourself regularly!

Be kind when it comes to you. Of all emotions, love is easily spread and attracted.

When I give lectures on self-love, people ask me, how to love themselves and what is the whole self-love process? I suggest them to take care of themselves, and then not to push themselves very hard. Try to have a good sleep daily, spare yourself some time for meditation and exercise. Learn to say no, if you don't want to do something. Go for regular body massage and spa. Shop for yourself. Take care of your mental and physical health by going on some vacations. These are some ways of loving yourself and feeling positive.

Be yourself even when the world tries to tame you, run free and wild. The right people will run right along with you and then you will see everything else will fall into place and you will start rising. Repetition is the key to success. If you want to love yourself, then give positive affirmations to yourself every day.

In the later chapters, I will give you some affirmations, which will help you a lot.

The repetition of thought that you are good, in order to love yourself and the easiest step to feel good and happy is to focus on the small details of what you are thinking, feeling and doing. Question yourself on whether it is a positive attitude which is making you happy and positioning you on high vibration or it is a negative perspective which is making you sad, depressed and low.

By thinking through new perspectives, in terms of feelings and actions, there is an added advantage of a sense of progress. It also provides a 'fine-grained feedback'. You will feel that your happiness level is improving.

Habits are made up of many little thoughts, such as feelings and actions. Paying attention to the little changes in thoughts, feelings and actions will help you to achieve a sense of progress, even if you have not fully formed a new habit yet.

This progress is your friend, no matter how small it is. Moreover, any new habit takes twenty-one days to replace the old one.

When you focus on all the little thoughts, feelings and actions while building a new habit, then it provides you more scaffolding to hold your habit in place and gradually this habit of yours will find its root deep in your subconscious mind.

> *"You are the special unique child of the almighty, you yourself as much as anybody in the entire universe, deserve your love and affection."*

Simple Techniques to Raise Your Vibrations

"The key to success is realizing the power in you and using it daily towards your goal."

After making it a habit to be happy, now it's time to feel good. Here are some techniques through which you can raise your vibrations and energy levels.

Music

Music has the power to relax the mind and is a wonderful method of relieving stress and any unwanted thought. Putting on music that talks to your soul will instantly change your mood and lower your stress. Just listen to some good music that initiates love and makes you feel good, and relax your mind. Listen to music while you are working, driving, cooking and reading. You can put on some good music, sing your favorite song, just to enjoy music in solace. Music has been proved to stimulate brain waves (positivity comes from the resonance of the beats), which in turn changes your mood and even behavioral responses, depending on the type of music you are listening to. Classical music and soft binaural beats music are known to calm the mind by stopping the thoughts from messing up.

The music with positive affirmations is very effective in meditation; it will connect you to the higher self by raising your vibrations. It makes my mind calm and more productive.

Remember a sweet child

Children are such wonderful teachers! Think of a child you love and adore, think of her smile, her naughtiness, how pure he/she is. Uplift your mood by remembering how a child leads a life without stress and free from tensions of the future and the past. Children are the purest reflections of the essence of life in all its beauty. Children live in the present and flourish the present moment itself. It is only the heart that lives in the present moment, not the mind. The gift that children bring to us, is their heart and a pure soul. By offering their soul's purity to us, they invite our heart to come out and play; they invite our joyful and creative selves to dance in the present moment with them and all our life.

Pray

Spare a little time to pray and meditate. It builds a link between you and the almighty. Meditation makes a pattern of prayers in the subconscious mind, brings faith and lets our mind stay calm.

How to pray effectively

At first, what is a prayer? Prayer is a spiritual communication between a soul and the almighty, the universe, god or super soul, whatever you wish to call it. It constantly seeks for the gratitude that is felt in our heart. It ultimately connects our aura with god's.

To pray is to surrender each and everything to the almighty. It is all about feeling light and starting a beautiful conversation with the almighty. Prayer is to ask god and listen to what he wants to say.

It will seem tougher to those who are not aligned to the proper vibrational frequency. Always remember, god is not a limited identity, he has plenty of resources, which you can't even think of.

Some essential elements to pray effectively are:

surrender

Show gratitude

Ego-less soul

Pray for humanity
Ask for mercy
Have faith

Surrender

It means to set aside our own plans and surrender ourselves to god. Surrendering is letting go of our fears and doubts. It is like leaving each and everything on the almighty and asking for help. When we surrender our fears, our doubts and our inner being, we begin to feel light; our soul becomes free from worldly things. It's never about interfering in your daily routine or running away from one's responsibility.

It's about doing your regular tasks with the sense of responsibility as this is given to you to serve humanity and every human, the child of god. Surrendering also consists of forgiveness. When we forgive other's sins and also our own, then we are making our soul's aura clear and fresh.

Show gratitude

Gratitude is feeling thankful to the almighty for each and everything he has given us. Due to him, we are here on earth and he is feeding us well and he has great plans for in future as well. Be thankful for all the things god has given. It's the most effective step for effective prayers, but it needs to be done in full humility.

Ego-less soul

To become ego-less is to choose love. When we love unconditionally and have divine love in our mind for humanity, for whosoever we want to pray, then the ego vanishes. Love is the only remedy for ego.

The divine unconditional love is the purest form of the soul. Love soaks all ego from the heart and changes it into altruistic attitude, ultimately making the soul very pure.

Pray for humanity

When we pray for humanity, when we pray for each and every person, when we pray for all human beings for their well-being and for their happiness, we become an active part of the universe and whatever we give, we receive. The more love we put into the prayer, the more we will get. We free ourselves from unnecessary wishes and wills. With pure love for humanity, one can easily access the stage of surrender. Surrendering while praying rids us of fears and suspicion , by bringing together the soul and body into a single entity. Therefore, we should pray for one and all.

Ask for mercy

Ask the almighty for whatever you want and for whom you want. Asking is seeking help from the master of the universe. Asking in faith gives you proper reply to listen and to act. You will find ways to accomplish your tasks and have synchronous events to prove it.

Asking is seeking help from the almighty for your or any other's sufferings; the help which was definitely given to you, without any obstacles or any favour.

Have faith

Faith is the most important aspect of prayers. Actually, it's the basis of all the prayers and religions. When you trust anything blindly, the universe conspires to make your wishes and prayers to come true through immense faith.

Faith creates miracles. True faith will have all these qualities. It makes prayer more effective.

Reading

It really doesn't matter what book you read, but by losing yourself thoroughly into an engrossing book, you can escape from the worries and stresses of everyday world and spend a while exploring the domain of the author's imagination.

Reading good self-help books, affirmations, scriptures, always helps a person to stay calm and peaceful and it also puts back the feelings of loneliness.

Reading regularly not only makes you smarter, but also increases your brain power. Such transformational books provide knowledge through which someone can change their respective life.

Driving

Driving can be both, tiring and satisfying, depending on the circumstances. A journey without a destination is the best kind of journey. It not only makes you feel invincible, but courageous too. It gives better experiences and cultural understanding in order to enhance your knowledge. Go for a long drive, don't plan where to go, just explore the beauty spread over all around us by the almighty god.

Meditation

When you start meditating on a regular basis, you start gaining access to your inner self and the universe more than you had ever gained before. From your inner core, you can start visualizing vibrational energy. By meditating, you connect to the formless universe and can easily converse and associate yourself to anyone.

Start meditating every day and you will get better and better at your meditation as you gain experience. Don't be discouraged if you don't have strong visualizations right from the beginning of meditation.

I work in a bank. When I come back home in the evening, I feel totally exhausted and tired. To relieve myself from such tiredness and exhaustion, I lock my room for half an hour, listen to binaural beats and position myself in the most comfortable way. Then, I breathe in and out on the sound of the clock. This is just to make the mind calm and free it from any obstructing thoughts. Once my mind is free from other thoughts, it concentrates just on the sound of the beat, or the clock, and I come to know about the vibrational patterns around me and feel connected to them.

When we leave the thought process, we instruct our thoughts to let go of all fears, resentment, anger and jealousy.

Sound sleep

Sleep deprivation is the main source of all anxiety, depression, anger and sadness. So assure yourself to have a good sleep. The manifestation process is carried on while sleeping because our subconscious mind starts finding the way to manifest our dreams. That way, a sound sleep is a must. However, sleeping for more than 6-7 hours a day makes you lazy and less productive. The duration of sound sleep can be somewhat less or more then the prescribed time, but it should be uninterrupted and deep.

After coming to know about sound sleep, I used to sleep for approximately twelve hours. Isn't it hilarious and dangerous? Wasting half a day for sleep! Quality sleep is not in sleeping straight for ten hours or so. When the mind is adequately drowsy and body too feels the same burden, that's the exact time to sleep. To get rid of this habit, I started chanting mantras before sleeping and after waking up. It shaped my subconscious mind to not entertain unwanted thoughts.

The ten minutes before sleep and ten minutes after waking up are the most crucial times for manifestation. It is the time when your subconscious mind can easily change the old perception and old habits. This is the time when we can easily imbibe new habits into our subconscious. So chanting mantras like 'Simran', 'Om' or reciting affirmations at this time helps the most. It also strengthens the subconscious mind and leads to sound sleep.

Dance

The shortcut to happiness is nothing but dance. Dance is a wonderful way to connect to your inner self. It is perhaps one of the oldest and most widespread practices known to man, which not only fulfils our need for free expression and leisurely releases the worries, but also bridges a gap between the finite and infinite.

Dance is the easiest way to connect with the almighty. Play a song and start dancing. Imagine no one is watching you and your blood circulation will boost up, creating an immense energy in the body. The energy of atoms is spontaneous and creates high vibrations, and boosts up the mood. The higher energy levels of the body get matched with the high vibrations and consequently connect itself with the universe. A saying of Rumi is, "*Dance, when you're broken open. Dance, if you've torn the bandage off.*

Dance in the middle of fighting. Dance in your blood. Dance when you're perfectly free."

Washroom technique

This technique would although sound hilarious, but yet it works very well as experienced by me. As a banker, I sometimes experienced contempt by my boss who tried to pressurize me for targets and work. I always felt so exhausted and sometimes got depressed. When it was unbearable, I rushed to the washroom and started surfing my phone, saw the pictures of my kids, my husband, read some affirmations and prayed for just one second and boosted up my mood. With that, I got back in the high vibrational frequency and got relieved from all anxiety. Gradually, this task became a technique for me, and then, no one could easily lower my vibrations and I was always in the happy state and the arrival of favorable circumstances led to higher vibrations in me. The things that came to me were now of same vibrations. So, I didn't need to plan any manifestation, I started using my mind for thought processing and accomplishing things.

"Just think and it's already accomplished."

Every thought that you think is vibrating at a very personal frequency. It will now attract thoughts of the same frequency. Now, these two combined thoughts will attract another thought of the same frequency. This collection will attract another bunch of thoughts, until and unless it becomes powerful enough to attract 'real life situations' and manifestation. So basically, negativity will get you down and positivity will elevate your inner self and purify your aura.

> *"Thoughts create a chain; one positive thought attracts another positive thought and creates a chain of positive thoughts and vibrations. It works vice versa with the negative thoughts."*

Yoga Can Help You Relax And Calm Down

Stress and anxiety contaminate health and quality of life more than any other emotion. Stress has been compared to a slow-moving time bomb, which can alter the quality of your life. It can cause diabetes, blood pressure and heart disease in a healthy body, within a short span of time. The good news is that stress can be controlled and eradicated gradually by our own will. Since yoga works very well by awakening 'chakras' of the body. Therefore, it helps to reduce stress and anxiety.

Originated in India, yoga is one discipline in which the body and mind are conceived as a unit. Through the yogic postures (*asanas*) and the breathing (*pranayama*), our body is filled with energy and positivity. It also relaxes the muscular tension and the cells are stimulated.

Unlike other stress-reducing practices, yoga allows you to reduce not only the symptoms of stress, but also makes you aware of the cause of stress or anxiety. During performing yoga, our body releases accumulated tensions and reaches to a great state of relaxation. So, this influences our central nervous system as well as the circulatory, digestive and respiratory system. Yoga provides for relaxation, and that too, instantly. It also helps in recomposing the energy balance of the body, loosening and releasing tensions and contractures.

We are automated beings that contemplate life from the same prism. Our reactions and attitudes do not change since we are submerged in numerous cultural, social, educational and other constraints that limit our freedom of development.

To regulate and balance the functions of the body and mind, it is necessary to learn to economize the energy produced by the body, which very often is spent uselessly. More energy is employed in keeping muscles continually ready for action than in true action.

During relaxation, practically none of the *prana* (vital energy) is consumed. Other benefits include, decrease in anxiety and blood pressure, stabilization of cardiac and respiratory functions, improvement of blood circulation and quality of sleep, increased skin temperature, increased speed of reflexes and ability to concentrate and memory, as well as greater resistance to diseases and better cerebral oxygenation.

The practice of relaxation in a habitual and constant way also entails the increase of the creative capacity, and a greater capacity of learning also, the development of the level of consciousness, the capacity for direct internal visualization and reflection of the natural tendency. The key is *abhyasa* (constant practice), that is, integrating relaxation into everyday life.

Yoga to relax and calm down

Here are five yoga ways to combat stress, which are very easy to put into practice. Of course, these types of exercises can be carried out occasionally. Although, it is also worth practicing yoga as often as possible.

Child's Pose

Also, called *balasana*, this posture is perfect to combat stress as it is used in yoga classes to rest. Therefore, the child's posture provides mental rest and is mainly used to calm anxiety and general stress. Performing it is very easy: just kneel and place your upper body on the floor, with outstretch arms, inhaling and exhaling

Viparita karani

This posture is obtained by putting your legs on the wall. It is ideal for stress and back ailments. This is because this position decreases and relieves tension in the lower part of the spine and hip. Also, this posture is of great help in treating other types of aches and pains such as arthritis, insomnia, mild depression and cramps in various parts of the body.

Shavasana

The *shavasana* posture is one of the basic ways to relax and reduce stress. In broad outline, the body's posture relaxes the body, soothes the mind and relieves stress. This is used to treat anxiety, high blood pressure, depression and headaches. Although this posture seems simple, in truth it is not that simple. First of all, it requires being completely calm and focused.

Firstlie down on a mat facing upwards, with your legs open at hip height. Rest your arms on the sides, with the palms facing up. Then close your eyes and breathe deeply and slowly, while taking all the relaxation to the body in general. Concentrate. This position should be maintained for about five or ten minutes.

Closed-angle spine

This position helps in controlling stress and to have a better quality of life, especially in the emotional aspect. That is why this posture is very effective for anger and distress. The close-angle spine is performed as follows:

First, lie on your back, placing two small pillows on the side of each thigh. Then, place the soles of the feet facing each other.

The palms of the hands should be at the side of the body, looking up. Breathing should be slow and deep for one to two minutes. The knees should open and close while you are doing this posture.

Kapalabhati pranayama

This type of posture is one of the most well-known and easiest to perform. It helps mainly in relaxing the body and reducing stress and anxiety. In this case, it is enough to sit with knees bent and hands on the knees. A series of deep and regular breaths is maintained with closed eyes.

When you practice these *asanas,* you begin to understand and perceive what impact they have on your body and mind. Each movement releases stress and tension and after a few minutes, the state of your mind improves. So, now you are clearer and more relaxed than before. Your body is more composed and relaxed and you feel a deep state of joy and relaxation.

> *"A mind filled up of positive thoughts, body nourished by good food and exercise, heart and soul imbibe love and gratitude, lead to a successful life."*

2

Burning Desire

"There is one quality which one must possess to win, and that is definiteness of purpose, the knowledge of what one wants, and a burning desire to possess it."

–Napoleon Hill

A burning desire is the starting point of all accomplishments. As a little fire cannot give much heat, a weak desire cannot produce great results.

Desire is a powerful thought that initiates the process of 'law of attraction'. Desire is like asking the universe for something you want; it's a request you put in before the almighty in the form of prayer, demand, subconscious thoughts or visualization.

Desire is the thought that you really want in your subconscious and conscious mind. Nevertheless, you have to ask it from the universe through reaching for higher vibration.

Whatever we desire is a thought already created by the almighty. In order to ask it again from the almighty is the part of the process. It's the acknowledgement of the thought given to you by the universe. Ask and it will be given to you, seek and you will find, knock and the door will open for you.

Make a request to the formless universe, whatever you want in your life, whether it is good health, good business, good job, or good relationships, basically anything. Raise your vibrations and ask with an unshakeable faith and you will begin to see miracles happening around you.

If you want to know what god wants you to do, ask him and he will gladly tell you, for he is always ready to give a magnanimous supply of wisdom to those who ask him.

Now the question arises – how to get the thing? Moreover, how to know about true desires? What is your aim in life or the goal of your journey?

Start conversing with the almighty regularly. It is a step by step procedure and starts with the smallest of things. As you wake up, start asking simple questions like:

- What do I love to do the most?
- What should I wear today?
- In which dress do I look gorgeous?
- What are my plans for today?
- What will be the perfect food for me today?
- What should I do to make my beloved happy?
- How to impress my boss today?
- What plans should I make to succeed in my career?

- How can I achieve my goals?
- Enlighten the path from where I have to start accomplishing my dreams?
- What should I do to make my skin glow?

These regular routine questions would make you habitual to converse with the formless, the almighty. It will make the habit of asking, to make the request and to clear your mind. This is the process to know about your burning desire. When the formless universe will gives you the hints of the right path and the answer to your questions, then the outcomes will be visible. You will develop a sense of belief and faith.

> *"When there is a burning desire in you, it will never let you sleep, it will knock you everyday to wake up and fulfill your dreams."*

The power of writing

Anyone who wishes to improve the quality of their inner self, as well as their outer self, would do well to take out a piece of paper and start writing out their aims and desires. The moment your desires are written on paper, it is done. Natural forces and the universe will come into play that will start to transform these desires into reality.

By writing out your burning desires on paper, you create a clear picture in your subconscious mind about your aims and goals. It will be a clear indication to the subconscious mind that, this is the most important thought for you and it must be nurtured and should be on priority.

All the abundance is for you. The universe has sufficient amount of everything for everybody. So, never hesitate or never feel shy to put your desires before the almighty. There are no limits. All limits are for people who do not want to grow, but the almighty has an abundance of everything. All the limits are in the thoughts that you have nurtured. Raise your frequency and then you will see that you are limitless.

With god, there is no limit to what you can do. There is no obstacle that you can't overcome with him by your side. Everything is possible.

Austrian skydiver and daredevil Felix Baumgartner jumped from 128,100 feet above the earth's surface, smashing the previous records for the highest ever skydive and the highest manned balloon flight, to become the first person in history to break the speed of sound in a free dive.

Felix Baumgartner's skydive from 24 miles above the earth's surface was faster than the speed of sound. He jumped from stratosphere and broke all his limits.

That's why the famous author of the book The Alchemist, *Paulo Coelho writes:*

"Felix has landed safely after his jump from stratosphere. Never accept your limitations because there is no limitations viva Felix!!!"

Limitations are always in the mind. Limitations are always in the prayers and always in the demands, which stop you from being successful, which stop you from fulfilling your dreams. When you limit your demands, you stop yourself from dreaming big.

JUST DREAM BIG!

> *"Limited thoughts seek limited success, dream big and achieve big."*

If you don't ask, you will never get it. Writing your dreams is also a form of asking. If a child is thirsty in his school and he doesn't ask his teachers about it, then how can the teacher know and how can the child satisfy his thirst?

You have to ask, you have to request. If you just let your subconscious do the asking, the universe will listen and definitely answer you.

Request the almighty and let it go, leave it, leave that request on his omnipresence. He will definitely take care of your request and will guide you to the shortest possible path to fulfill it. The universe is a donor, a universal donor. If anyone looks for anything with a burning desire, god fulfills the desire, irrespective of the faults the human has.

A burning desire is the most fundamental aspect; if you don't master, that the law of attraction won't work in your life. Almost all the successful people have a burning desire to be successful. They practice their desire every day by praying, acting accordingly and visualizing. You must have a definite goal or a desire, which is so big, so all-encompassing, that you are excited and scared of it at the same time. When you have both the feelings simultaneously working for a single goal, consider that goal a limitless one. Stick to that goal and rest not until you achieve it.

Napoleon Hill, in his book Think and Grow Rich *has written:*

> *"I will burn all bridges behind me and stake my entire future on my ability to get what I want. Every person who wins in any undertaking must be willing to burn his ships and cut all sources of retreat. Only by doing so, can one be sure of maintaining that state of mind known as* burning desire to win, *essential for success."*

Give your immense loyalty and love to your desires and dreams. The desire should be very clear; it should not change frequently.

I would like to share a small story that was told by my father in my childhood. This story comes from the epic *Mahabharata*:

> *The story is about the Pandava brothers. The five brothers were known to be great warriors and were the prince of the kingdom. One day, their teacher tied an artificial bird on a branch of a tree. The teacher had told the Pandava brothers that they must aim at the bird's eye with their bow and arrow.*
>
> *The eldest brother Yudhisthira went first with his bow and arrow. When he was ready to shoot, the teacher asked him, "Son, what do you see?"*
>
> *Yudhisthira answered, "I see the sky, the bird and the tree."*
>
> *The teacher asked him to go back and he called upon the second one, Bhima. Again he asked, "Son, what do you see?" Bhima answered, "I see the tree, the branches, leaves, and the bird".*

Once again, the teacher told Bhima to step back. At last, it was Arjuna's turn.

Arjuna stepped forward to position himself with his bow and arrow.

The teacher asked, "Son, what do you see?"

Arjuna said what guru Drona was wanting to hear from all the princes, "The eye".

The teacher was now beaming with self-satisfaction and pride. He said; "Shoot my son, shoot!"

Arjuna was later known to be among the best archers of the world.

The moral of the story is to concentrate on the burning desire and nothing else. The first two brothers were distracted by the other things they saw. For instance, the sky, the bird, the tree, the leaves, etc. But, Arjuna was not distracted when he looked towards the target; all he saw was the bird's eye and then the whole universe conspired with him to achieve his target. Therefore, to fulfill your dreams, you should be very clear in your mind. Never be distracted and have deep faith in yourself, that you can achieve it. You need to stay focused on your goals with a pure conscience.

Clarity of mind means clarity of passion, too.

Clear minds love their desires and dreams very intensely.

The creation process is all about feeling good, with a high vibrational state. Request to the formless universe and if you have that burning desire in your heart, your request will be granted. The formless almighty is omnipresent. Feel and believe his presence; request him what you want with a burning desire and your manifestation will start bearing fruit. Now, your desire has become your action. Every day, you have to evoke that desire and work on it, to think how to achieve it. All it needs is a burning desire in you to achieve your dream.

> *"A burning desire in your heart with a limitless approach, and a clear vision to your goal, will make you eligible to achieve that desire."*

3

Visualization

"Visualization is the nexus that joins the spiritual and the physical worlds."

–Peter Kummer (German Psychologist)

Close your eyes. Ask someone to read these sentences for you or read it and try to visualize it.

Imagine yourself sitting in your bedroom. The room is calm and cool. Suddenly, someone comes into your room with a plate in which a lemon is placed. You cut the lemon and put some salt on it. You squeeze the salted lemon juice on your tongue and feel the taste of sour lemon.

Now stop!

Now, just feel. Is your mouth watering?

Am I right?

There is no lemon and salt here, but still the saliva to digest the lemon comes into your mouth. This is because of the power of thoughts and deep visualization. Our body cells work on our thought process and our mind. Now, you have seen the effect of visualization with this one-minute experiment.

The basic idea behind visualization is that if you want to get what you want in your life, you have to create a detailed picture of that desire in your mind. It is simply a mental rehearsal where you create images in your mind for achieving your goal or doing whatever you want. When you generate these images again and again, the subconscious mind starts viewing it as real and it acts upon the images you construct within. However, you need to know that it isn't through visualizing that you actually create. Rather, emotions and feelings are linked to the images you visualize, producing a penultimate effects.

The emotions linked to the visualization take you to the same vibrational frequency as of your desire.

The key to mental visualization lies in the ability to link emotions, sensations and feelings. It is a process similar to daydreaming. For some people, this might look like magic, but there is no magic involved. Only the natural processing of the power of thoughts, subconscious mind and natural mental laws create this magic of positivity. When you visualize your goal, i.e. the image, you elevate your frequency, bringing your energy in line with the image or particular desire that you want to achieve desperately.

The ability to visualize is not attained by just desiring. Constant and patient training with proper action over a period of time with persistent action results in visualization. So, lots of efforts and practice are required to attain it.

Whatever you request from the universe for fulfillment, you have to create a clear picture in your subconscious mind. Now, this image will interact with the universe, even if you have fallen asleep. Now, you don't have to think about it all the time; you don't have to bother yourself with this tiresome thought. You have activated your subconscious mind to do the task for you.

Imagination is the beginning of creation. You imagine what you desire, you will get what you imagine and at last, you find that goal.

If you want to be an actor, just start imagining the same. For that purpose, start practicing your roles, start giving autographs, start behaving like an actor and inhabit that imagination in every task you do. This would serve as a regular request to the universe that you have full faith in the almighty, that your wishes will come true. The most important thing which should be remembered is that visualization only works when your feelings and emotions are attached to it. Imagine with all your senses, and what you dream will become reality. See the image in your mind, listen to the sounds, taste it, smell it, and feel it in your body.

It is already written in Srimad Bhagwat Geeta – *creation is only projection of something that already exists. So, whatever you desire, you imagine, is already there in the universe. Its existence was always there. Let's imagine you want to live on any other planet, which means there is another planet and that's true.*

There are planets, solar systems, and galaxies. If one starts speaking to them, there is no limit, no end. There are so many worlds on so many planets which he has created. They are existent upon his command. The almighty watches all his creations and rejoices.

Imagine your life the way you want it to be, imagine everything you want, take your imagination with you every day. Imagine what it would be like if your relationships were all fantastic, imagine how your life would be if you had all the money you needed. Imagine how you would feel had you been fired from your job. This world is just a canvas of your imagination. Whatever you want, just paint it through your imagination and visualization.

You should know that when you complete your part of the creation, it's entirely a different world for you. You begin to feel happy, and you feel good now and then. This new world contains everything you want, even if you don't see it. You have to know that you will definitely find it.

I read a great example of visualization and the power of thoughts on Wikipedia. It's about Caroly Takas.

> *He was a sergeant in the Hungarian army and a world best shooter (pistol). During his training in 1938, a defective grenade blew up on his right hand, which was his dominating hand, and that caused loss of his right forearm. But despite that, he didn't stop. Determination was there in his imagination and he regularly visualized it in his mind.*
>
> *After spending a month in the hospital, he started practicing shooting with his left hand – the non-dominating hand.*
>
> *In early 1939, he went for Hungary National Championship, where other participants offered him sympathy, but he stunned everyone after winning the*

championship by shooting with his left hand. After that, he won a gold medal in the Olympics too. Winning gold at Olympics was his final dream. He went through tragedy and triumph; he was the coach and mentor for other Hungarian Olympians, who also got shooting honours.

Through your ability to visualize, imagine and feel, you have dominance over all creations.

The following normal incident from my life will prove how fast imagination, visualization and love work.

I love to eat langar (the food distributed after the spiritual congregation as a holy gift in India).One Sunday, I was feeling like it had been a long time that I had eaten langar, especially the particular dal and aloo-gobhi. I thought this and left, and forgot what I had thought. Suddenly, my husband called me that we had to go to attend a marriage at my mother's place and I would be staying at my mother's place. When I reached my mother's place, I got to know that a lot of langar had been left over due to the evening congregation, so, she didn't make any food that day. My mother asked should she cook something else for me or I would be okay with the langar. My little dream was coming true, so how could I resist it?

And then I ate the langar, which was exactly the same pulses and the same vegetable, and the same taste which I had imagined in the morning. It had the same flavour. I ate that langar with immense love and gratitude for the universe for accomplishing my little dreams and desires.

Best way to increase visualization: Meditation

"There must be meditation. Meditation is essential. Meditate!

Meditation is the best approach to spiritual life. That is the moment when we no longer are material when the soul is thinking about itself, when we are free of all materialistic worry; this is the marvelous moment when we are in touch with our soul."

–Swami Vivekananda

Robert Collier stated in *The New Thought* about the power of meditation – *knowing that you have to work with you a force, which never yet has failed in anything it has undertaken, you can go ahead in the confident knowledge that it will not fail in your case, either.*

So, to increase your visualization powers, start meditating every day and you will get better and better at your meditation as you gain experience. Don't be discouraged if you don't have strong visualizations right away.

The idea with meditating is to completely empty the brain, pause your thoughts and be calm from inside out. You just start focusing on breathing – breathe in, breathe out – and let your mind do whatever it wants to do, naturally. When you leave the thought process, you instruct your thoughts to let go of all fears, resentment, anger and jealousy. Therefore, you attract informative vibrations through deep breathing and also the blood circulation gets increased to raise the overall energy level of the body.

The naturalist and spiritual therapist, Peter Ragnar describes the process of deep breathing as, *the stimulation of the first cranial nerve, when air enters the nasal passage at the base of the cerebrum where the olfactory nerves end, produces vivid mental images. Regular practice of deep breathing eliminates the factors that distort the understanding of our consciousness*.

Deep breathing stimulates the visualization process and controls it consciously. It also links you with the formless universe and provides you with extra sensorial information from the universe, for instance, telepathy and psychic powers.

Meditation will put you in a relaxed open state, which allows your visualization and imagination to penetrate you on a deeper level.

Relaxing the mind will help keep your mind calm and clear out any negative thoughts, perceptions fears, and doubts that hold you back from achieving your dreams and desires.

Visualization through meditation is more of a by-product; the main product is something else. When you start meditating on a regular basis, you gain access to your inner self and the super soul more than you ever had before. From that inner self, you start experiencing strong visualizations.

Visualize the universe which is full of energy, love and compassion. This universe will convey all your messages, your feelings and also your love to the other person; this process is termed as 'telepathy'. Universe helps in visualization; it is super powerful and is the only thread which connects each and every soul to itself.

To start meditation, create a time table to meditate. You can start with just five minutes and can extend the time gradually.

While meditating, you must not force any thought or image into your head. Start by focusing on breathing, and let your mind do whatever it wants to do naturally.

Robin Sharma in his book *The Monk Who Sold His Ferrari* suggests meditation by the "Heart of Rose" technique. In this technique, you have to concentrate on a rose and think about it only, for instance, its colour, leaves or thorns and practice it daily to concentrate your mind and to think only about the particular object. It means obstructing other thoughts to come and interfere.

With this technique, you will start focusing on a goal and all those opposing thoughts will stop interfering through practicing meditation.

You will have strong visualizations just by 'letting go' and allowing your brain to put on the show. These visualizations will produce great insight into your mind because they are not constructed manually; rather they just occur on their own.

Visualization with persistent action

Always remember that visualization is not magic. You still have to put in the effort and do some persistent actions while you are on your path to achieving your goal.

All information is vibration until the cerebrum processes it as an image inside our minds.

Jim Carrey once stated in an Oprah Show, that *visualization works if you work hard*. That's the thing. You can't just visualize and then go make a sandwich. Constant efforts and action are always required.

Boxing legend Muhammad Ali, one of the greatest sportspersons the world has ever known, always visualized his victory , even when the actual fight was yet to happen.

One of the reasons for Ali's success as a boxer was that he was a believer in the process and effects of visualization. Ali used to rehearse mentally every fight many times before stepping into the ring. He would see himself at the end of a fight with his arms aloft and the referee declaring him the winner of the match. He would imagine listening to the crowd chanting his name and celebrating his victory.

He paid much attention to the detailing of his visualization and used to strengthen his weaknesses through predictions before the fight. He would tell his opponent, when he was going to win the fight. He even predicted the round in which he would be declared the winner. He was extremely well prepared when he stepped into the ring, both physically and mentally. He had already won the fight in his mind; he would direct all his focus and energy on making this a reality. He would give his subconscious mind an instruction to find ways to help him make his visions come true.

Muhammad Ali not only lived his life with a strong sense of vision, but also with intention strong enough to lead him towards success in his career. He said that champions aren't made in gyms, champions are made from something they have deep inside them – a desire, a dream and a vision. They have to have the skill and the will, and the will must be stronger than the skill.

Similarly, in basketball, Michael Jordan always visualized the last shot in his mind before he took one in real life. He said that every time he felt tired while exercising and training, he closed his eyes to see that picture, to see that list with his name on it. This motivated him to do baskets while the game was on.

Visualization can easily be interrupted by negative thoughts and have enough power to spoil the dreams

Reject negative thoughts

Negativity not only makes positive thoughts difficult to incur, but also stops positivity and blocks the thoughts of action.

To stop negativity, you have to pay attention to what you are thinking the whole day and have to deeply analyze your thoughts. Sometimes, past unpleasant thoughts will randomly come into your mind.

You have to take care of those thoughts.

Whenever I come across such situations, I immediately ask my subconscious mind to get rid of those thoughts.

When we stop one negative thought, then the chain stops by default, and it blocks the pool of negativity which lies further.

Let us imagine that you are going to undergo a surgery, if you consider yourself lucky enough to be in the hands of a good surgeon, you are a positive thinker. If you learn everything about the surgery, the process, the team and how the surgery will undergo and what are the side effects, etc., you will start having thoughts of action. If you will start worrying about the outcome of the surgery, you will harbour negative thoughts. This is where the power of your subconscious mind will be checked. As soon as negativity comes into your mind, order it to stop and start thinking any pleasant thought. You only have to observe negative thoughts and when you find one, can't just try to restrict it from coming again, but give it a strong reason to go forever.

Negative thoughts always accompany fear with them. Fear is a primary defense and survival mechanism of all the living beings, which help us to avoid danger in taking risks. The negative thing about fear is, when it comes with intensity, it paralyzes your thoughts, weakens your immune system and stops your action.

When you are afraid of your future, that means you are not living in the present. When I personally analyzed the fear concept, I came to know about a simple cause of fear, that is 'attachment'.

When you are attached with someone or something ardently, so much that you can't live without it, it creates a fear of losing. Be it a relation, an entity, a job or anything in life. If you have detachment from these things, then you will never be caged in the prison of fear.

Let's imagine: you are having a sound job and your boss asks that you have to do a certain work, otherwise he will fire you from the job. If you will feel attached to the company, fear will arise out of nowhere and you will do the work, even it is not meant for you. Nevertheless, if you don't feel attached or you don't have any expectation, you shall have no fear. It will just be about money, which you can also find by working somewhere else. You will not let fear enter into your mind, which will result in strengthening your subconscious mind and your aura.

This is just an example, but in your daily life, fear attacks randomly. Lowering your vibrations means you are attached to the outcomes of your doing. So whenever you feel fear in your mind, analyze it, find a solution or the second option for that. Visualize the outcomes of your actions and you shall have no fear at all. Pray to the almighty and he will guide you. This technique will immediately stop negative thoughts and make your mind calm so that you can think of a solution in peace.

Actually, fear is an illusion, it is not real at all, but courage is eternal and cannot die. Concentrate on your courage and fear will disappear.

> *"Fear is an illusion; the base of each fear is just the fear."*

4

The Belief System

"I tell you the truth, if ye have faith as small as a mustard seed, you can say to this mountain, move from here to there and it will move, nothing will be impossible for you."

–Matthew 17:20 (New Testament)

Faith is the bridge between a desire and its accomplishments. You cannot get anything from the almighty or the universe if you ask for something, but do not really believe that you will receive it. It does not work this way.

You have to strongly believe that you are about to get what you want. In fact, try to convince yourself that you already have got what you want. This will give you an advantage because you will have an abundant state of mind, rather than thoughts of lack and scarcity. This will be hard to do if you are just starting off, so you should start by visualizing smaller desires.

At first, it will be much easier to believe that you already possess small desires. Once you manifest them, you can move on to bigger ones because you will be more assured that your desires are being responded to by the almighty. If you send a wish to the universe but you don't believe that you are already having your desire, your manifestation may not turn into reality because you approach the universe with the mindset of inadequacy. So, be careful about your belief and start manifesting from small things. You should completely open yourself and surrender to the almighty.

You need to trust the almighty, without trying to find out how to love things, how can you be so sure about getting that very love from him?

Leave this job to the formless almighty; do not try to involve yourself in the manifestation process. Just trust the universe and it will bring the desired love in the most perfect and unexpected way.

Here, a thought strikes me, which is the law of gestation.

The Law of Gestation states that everything has a gestation period, during which it develops. Just like a seed gestates in the womb of mother earth for a particular time period, any creative process and each transition we experience also has a period of gestation and that is a necessary part of the process.

So, if we become impatient and have no belief, we will pluck the seed out of the soil every day and will still hope for the seed to grow; which is not possible.

Self-trust is the first secret to success. At first, you have to believe in yourself. Birds sitting on the branch of a tree don't scared of the shaking branch due to wind, because the birds have faith on their wings. So, believe in yourself; as devotion means self-trust and self-trust means trust and belief in the almighty.

A child was sitting in an airplane. Suddenly, there was an announcement for emergency landing. All the passengers were scared, but that little child had a smile on his face. A passenger asked him how he didn't feel any fear?

The reply from the child was, "My father is flying this plane and I know he won't let anything happen to me."

This is belief.

The same situation is applicable to us as well. Our father, the almighty is with us; so whatever the circumstance, he will always be good to us. Don't be afraid. Just believe. Believing the unknown is the greatest power which you can possess.

I am sharing a real story of my student, Ruhani. She wanted to get a good job but whenever she went for an interview, she always got rejections. One day, she was standing in my institute and started crying. But her eyes were full of faith and belief. Her words were: "God, I need a job. if you won't give me a job, then my parents would force me to get married, and I don't want to marry so soon. Dear almighty, I know you can do it and I know you will. In fact, you have to do it. It is your duty to decide what is good and what is bad for me. If I have wished something which cannot be granted, then you will show me an alternative. I know you can do anything. I know nothing is impossible for you. Don't know how? But I know you will grant my wish."

Within ten days from that incident, she got a job in Coimbatore, and from there, she shifted to Pune, and now she is living a very good life. All of this, with an unshakeable faith which is manifesting so many things such as her beloved, a beautiful daughter, a new job, also a new business running side by side, along with her job. All these incidents took place as she had faith, which does not know the way, but only knows the destination.

> *"Belief is something which can be seen in your eyes while praying."*

Belief formula

Belief formula is how to make a particular belief in your subconscious mind. After learning this, you can easily replace your old belief with a new one.

Belief is a combination of perception, evidence and repetition, within a certain time period.

Perception+Evidence+Repetition+Time=Belief

Perception

The current perception is what you think of yourself at any particular time. For example, you might believe that you are not an intelligent person. That's the perception you have about yourself at this particular time.

Evidence

The evidence you have gathered over the years to prove that perception might be that you failed in your exams in the past, you felt stupid around other people and other people may have said that you weren't particularly intelligent and so on. Your subconscious mind has gathered all this evidence to prove your perception and created a faith in which you believe by default.

Repetition

Over the months and years, you have repeatedly reminded yourself, and there may have been some repetitive failures which proved why you are not intelligent. So, your mind just assumes that you are not intelligent and the belief has found its root deep inside you.

Time

This is about the time since when you are holding this belief. The longer you hold a belief, the more you believe it. So if you have told yourself for years that you are not intelligent, undoubtedly you will think so for now as well.

That's how a belief is formed. Similarly, when you have empowering belief that has been formed by using the same formula – you believe that you are intelligent, you have gathered evidence over the years to prove that and you have repeated that belief over the years, then you are intelligent. There shouldn't be any doubt that you are intelligent.

When I was six years old, my paternal aunt gave birth to a son and named him 'Sumit'. After two months, I got news from my mom that my maternal aunt had also given birth to a baby boy. I just requested and didn't say to anyone, but the almighty, that please name this new baby boy also 'Sumit'. The very next day, I got news that they had named the baby as per my request to the almighty.

This is a small evidence on my perception that whatever I say or request to the almighty, it will definitely be fulfilled. It will happen steadily due to repetition and timing. From here, I got an unshakeable faith that could manifest anything.

If you believe, you will receive whatever you ask for in your prayer. To believe is to be powerful. Therefore, whatever you ask for in a prayer, believe that you have received it and it will be yours. Believing itself will create a miracle.

Dr Mark, a well-known cancer specialist, was once on his way to an important conference in another city where he was going to get an award for his service in the field of medical research. He was very excited to attend the conference and was desperate to reach as soon as possible. He had worked long and hard on his research and felt his efforts deserved this award.

However, two hours after the plane took off, the plane made an emergency landing at the nearest airport due to some technical issue. He was scared that he wouldn't make it in time for the conference. Dr Mark immediately went to the reception and found that the next flight was scheduled after ten hours. The receptionist suggested him to rent a car and drive himself down to the conference city which was only four hours away.

Having no other choice, he agreed to the idea despite his hatred for driving long distances. Dr Mark rented a car and started his journey. However, soon after he left, the weather suddenly changed and a heavy storm began to form. The rain made it very difficult for him to see and he missed a turn he was supposed to take.

After two hours of driving, he was convinced he was lost. Driving in the heavy rain on a deserted road, feeling hungry and tired, he frantically began to look for any sign of civilization. After some time, he finally came across a small tattered house. He was desperate; he got out of the car and knocked on the door. A beautiful lady opened the door. He explained the matter and asked her if he could use her telephone.

However, the lady told him that she did not have a phone or any electronic gadget, but told the doctor to come inside and wait until the weather improved. Hungry, wet and exhausted, the doctor accepted her kind offer and walked in. The lady gave him hot tea and something to eat. The lady told him that he could join her for prayer. Nevertheless, Dr Mark smiled and said that he believed in hard work only and told her to continue with her prayers.

Sitting on the table and sipping the tea, the doctor watched the woman in the dim light of candles as she prayed next to what appeared to be a small baby crib.

Every time she finished a prayer, she would start with another one. Feeling that the woman might be in need of help, the doctor seized the opportunity to speak as soon as she finished her prayers. The doctor asked her what exactly she wanted from god and enquired if she thought god would ever listen to her prayers. He further asked about the small child in the crib for whom she was apparently praying. The lady gave a sad smile and said that the child in the crib was her son who was suffering from a rare type of cancer and there was only one doctor named Mark who could help her with the treatment, but she did not have money to afford his fee. Moreover, Dr Mark lived in another far-off town. She said that god had not answered her prayer so far, but said that god would create some way out one day and added that she would not allow her fears to overcome her faith.

Stunned and speechless, Dr Mark was in tears rolling down his cheeks. He whispered 'god is great' and recollected the sequence of events. There was malfunction in the plane, a thunderstorm hit and he lost his way; and all of this happened because god had not just answered her prayer, but also gave the doctor a chance to come out of a materialistic world and give some time to poor helpless people who had nothing but rich prayers and unwavering faith.

So this is how unwavering faith can move mountains. The lady in the story had been praying for long. She had passed her period of gestation and left everything on god. She didn't know how it would be possible. I don't know if this story is true or fictional, but it teaches us a great lesson.

> *"Faith is the shortest possible path between you and god."*

Now the last step in making belief is;

Letting go

Letting go of the outcome is extremely important. You should not think or dwell on your desire again, as now it's time for you to trust the magical process. Believe that it is working and your desire is being processed and then let go of all the worries.

It means that instead of fighting with the almighty, fight for faith. It means, instead of complaining to the almighty, you thank him because your faith doesn't change anything around you, but it changes everything within you. Faith doesn't always shine and sparkle, but it helps you live through darkness and pain.

I was thirty years old when I gave my last exam of IBPS PO, government banking jobs for officers. I knew that this was my last chance according to the eligibility. I also knew that I would clear the exam, but when the interviews would come, I might cross the eligibility criteria. At that moment, I was in my academy with my staff and said, "I did my karma. I prepared well. I gave my exam well and now it's the work of the almighty to give me local posting and see the age criteria." After that, I let go the outcome, and never thought about that, because I knew whatever would happen, would be for my good. After a few months I got a joining letter to join in May, surpassing all the eligibility criteria. Just pray, do your karma and leave, let it go…

Let go and let in god

I'm sharing some life events and messages of Abraham Lincoln here, about his unwavering faith. The following messages, in Lincoln's own words, teach why looking to god should be as important to you today as it was to him then.

On 30 March 1863, President Lincoln proclaimed a national day of prayer and fasting to be held the next month. He explained:

> *"We have been the recipients of the choicest bounties of heaven; we have preserved these many years in peace and prosperity; we have grown in numbers, wealth and power as no other nation has ever grown. But we have forgotten god. We have forgotten the gracious hand which has preserved us in peace and multiplied and enriched and strengthened us, and we have vainly imagined, in*

the deceitfulness of our hearts, that all these blessings were produced by some superior wisdom and virtue of our own. It behooves us, then, to humble ourselves before the offended power, to confess our national sins and to pray for clemency and forgiveness."

Trust in his timing.

Lincoln had learned these principles over a lifetime of challenges, failures, and successes.

> *"Expect it, believe it and trust that it will come, our doubts are traitors, make us lose the good, we oft might win."*

5

Magic of Gratitude

"If the only prayer you said in your whole life was "Thank You", that would suffice."

–Meister Eckhart (1260 AD – 1328 AD), Christian writer and theologian

Gratitude is a powerful exercise for abundance in life. It raises your vibration and brings you into harmony with the energy of the universe. Gratitude can immediately transform all areas of your life.

No matter how bad someone's life may be, there is always something to be grateful for. As soon as they find it, their life will improve.

See the life you want as already existing.

See your life expanding in all areas.

Feel alive and joyful as things are moving quickly to make your life even more magnificent!

This is an emotional feeling you can tune in anytime and anywhere. It's the connection between you and the universe. I would say it creates and develops a connection of your soul with the super soul, the supreme power.

Gratitude acknowledges connections and perhaps, due to this reason, all spiritual guides link humans to gratitude.

You have connected yourself to the creative energy of the formless almighty already. No matter how your life looks, you have the power to make it better. This knowledge alone should inspire you to be grateful and to appreciate everything around you, for whatever you have or everything that is coming to you.

Gratitude is the most passionate transformative force in the universe. If you give five gifts as thanks every day, in twenty-one days you may not look at your life in the same way as you are looking now.

You should thank for some beautiful gifts that he has given to you without asking. Be it the food you eat, the breaths you take, sound sleep you have, beautiful hands or pretty eyes to see the beauty with, and everything that you are doing. Are you grateful to be alive each day or do you take your life for granted?

You cannot exercise much power and strength without gratitude because it is gratitude that keeps you connected with powers of the universe.

How can you expect to receive more good things if you don't appreciate what you already have?

What about giving gifts? When you give gifts, you should be giving without expectations of receiving something in return. However, the recipients need to feel grateful and should acknowledge your gift. If they express their gratitude then you will be likely to give them more gifts in the future. On the other hand, if they are ungrateful or do not acknowledge your generosity or never thank you, then you may decide not to give them anything else, because they are ungrateful.

So, in the same way, if you constantly express gratitude for what you have, the almighty will be happy to shower better things on you, just because you are grateful to him.

We have seen so many miracles that have taken place in field of health, wealth, and relationships. Where there is no hope, only with the grace of gratitude everything is recovered. Gratitude is the highest expression of love. It is a bridge of love. As you feel grateful, you feel good; you become happy and in turn raise your vibrations to higher frequency. That's how it can transform your dreams and your wishes.

Every time you feel grateful, you are giving love to the almighty and you reap what you sow. To have abundance of wealth, you should start appreciating each and every single penny you are having right now, or had in the past, and then start visualizing the wealth that you are going to have in your future.

Say 'thank you' to the almighty for the abundance, feel happiness and grateful from inside and send a lot of love to him.

Before eating, express your gratitude to god for he has given you your daily bread. When you wake up in the morning, you should be thankful for a sound sleep the previous night. You should show gratitude for all the beautiful things around you, like the sun, trees, farms, birds, animals and even the air. Also be thankful for all the materialistic things that the almighty has given to you. And just saying 'thank you' verbally doesn't work;

you have to feel it in the core of your heart. To be grateful is a powerful force to attract abundance in your life.

Simple gratitude exercises

1. Four questions daily:

Ask these four questions to yourself every day before sleeping, as it's a great way to bring things that you are grateful for to the forefront of your mind.

- What touched me today?
- Who or what inspired me today?
- What made me smile today?
- What's the best thing that happened today?

Answer these questions every day and write down in your gratitude journal, or you can use your phone's note.

Before going to bed each night, write a list of five things about that day for which you're grateful. Some days you will have exciting things to write down, and some days you will be writing down simple joys. Making a commitment to writing down good things each day makes it more likely that we will notice good things as they happen.

2. Grace before meals

Pausing in gratitude before eating doesn't have to be religious. It's a simple habit that helps us notice and appreciate the blessing of food on the table.

Giving thanks before each meal recognizes all of the people whose hard work was necessary for you to have food on your table. Everyone from the farmer who grew the food, the grocery store persons who stocked the shelves at your local grocery store, the person who cooked the meal and also the person who earned the money to bring that food for you, and last but not the least, gratitude towards the almighty, for the perfect atmosphere, perfect trees and perfect circumstances for the food to be served on your table.

It's a moment to pause and be mindful, as well as feel blessed that you have all the food and nourishment that you need.

3. Gratitude letter

Write a letter to someone who has exerted a positive influence in your life, but whom you have not thanked properly. This can be a teacher or a mentor from your past, a friend, a grandparent, or anyone else who helped you in some way.

The letter should contain your deep emotional feeling of gratitude and thanks. When I write my gratitude letter towards someone, my eyes fill with tears due to deep thankfulness.

I write how it feels and how their help has affected me at that time and now.

This practice will open your heart chakra very easily as at that time you are sending love and appreciation to the person who once helped you, means you are vibrating on a higher energy than before.

If you are an introvert and feeling uncomfortable to express your feeling to someone in writing, then there is no need to post or deliver your letter to that person. The vibrations are strong, your messages will definitely be conveyed through the universe to them.

4. A joy jar

A joy jar is basically a jar full of gratitude. All you need for this is a jar, some pieces of different colored papers and a pen. Make a daily practice to write on a paper one single thing for which you are grateful. After a week, read all your gratitude notes and feel them again and again. It's the simplest way to remind you the things you have taken for granted. After practicing this for just twenty-one days, you will generate a habit of finding good and appreciable things in others and in the nature around you. I put some money in that jar and give that to someone who is in need, with lots of gratitude.

According to Rhonda Byrne, author of *The Secret*: *"Gratitude is a great multiplier."*

Research shows that gratitude heightens the quality of life and induces happiness.

Two psychologists, Michael McCollough of Southern Methodist University in Dallas, Texas, and Robert Emmons of the University of California at Davis wrote an article about an experiment they conducted on gratitude.

They did this practice to see the impact of gratitude on humans. Several hundred people were divided into three different groups and all the participants were asked to keep daily diaries and journals.

The first group kept a diary of the events that occurred during the day without being told specifically to write about either good or bad things. The second group, however, was told to record their unpleasant experiences; and the last group was instructed to make a daily list of things for which they were grateful.

The results of the study indicated that exercising gratitude daily resulted in higher reported levels of alertness, enthusiasm, determination, optimism and energy. In addition, those in the gratitude group experienced less depression and stress, were more likely to help others, exercised more regularly, so became healthier and made greater progress toward achieving their personal goals.

How do the people feel the whole day when something good happens in a day?

Happiness levels increase and suddenly something bad happens, and the level comes down as the happiness level also comes down. So, in order to achieve the state of happiness, you must acknowledge the gifts of god and must thank him.

In India, we know it by the name of *'sehaj'* and *'saral'*. Simple, easy and effortless stage of mind and heart. It only comes when you practice gratitude daily. When gratitude emerges in your subconscious mind and soul, happiness and effortless contentedness arises in your mind and soul.

Expressing gratitude makes you feel connected. Many people in your life have helped you in one way or another. So, being grateful to them will not do you any harm.

When something good happens to you in a day, say thanks; when you come across a labour, say thank you to him. The universe may have conspired with him to build the roads, the flyovers, the bridges, the buildings for you, so say thanks to every single and small thing in your life. It will multiply the things you already have.

So, understanding and implementing the attitude of gratitude into your day to day life will help you to attract more good things into your life to be grateful for, and you will be able to get everything you want to have, be everything you want to be, and do everything you want to do.

You only have to make the practice to sleep and wake up with gratitude.

In the concept of law of attraction, gratitude masters every attribute of it. But the toughest part of being grateful is to feel it. It is to feel and have emotions of being grateful and have the deep power of love in the heart.

Do you ever notice, many people fail to show their pure and true gratitude towards the almighty because their gratitude lacks feelings and emotions?

The easiest way I discovered to show gratitude and love is to see the almighty everywhere and feel the divine presence and his love everywhere. See and feel the almighty in the air; you are breathing, be grateful for that. See the almighty in the trees, they give us oxygen, food, wood and many other things. Be grateful to the planet earth for she gave you shelter to live, food to eat and clothes to wear.

See god in every human being as everyone is a part of the super soul. Everyone has a soul which can connect to the almighty any time.

Everyone serves the planet through their love, their deeds and their presence. Be grateful to everyone for their love, which they are showering upon other creations of the creator.

When you start to feel the presence of the almighty in every human being, then everything, every creation and unconditional love will boost up. Thus, true gratitude is given to the almighty, so that you become a magnet of love, peace and happiness.

> *"Gratitude is the catalyst to speed up the law of attraction."*

6

Power of Forgiveness

"Take heed to yourselves; if your brother sins, rebuke him, and if he repents, forgive him."

–Luke 17:2-4 (New American Standard)

Forgiveness is a part of the process of healing and letting go of the past. In all the virtues, forgiveness is one of the hardest to put into practice. Lack of forgiveness or building a shell around yourself is a result of spiritual pride.

If you want happiness in your life, you must forgive everyone and everything in your life, for which you feel hurt.

Forgiveness is a medicine of your severe pain.

Your heart can be so deep and painful that somehow you need to justify it with both anger and hatred against those who caused it. You can come to believe that all kinds of falsehood can spread them in order to get revenge and to feel justified. But in fact, you must live in the world where forgiveness does not exist, and you use this justification to promote your own ego named as 'self-respect'. Most importantly, anger and hatred are the most disturbed emotions and lead to physical and medical illness.

Life always forgives you, as when you cut your finger. The subconscious intelligence, the formless soul within you sets about immediately to repair it. New cells build bridges over the cut. If you burn your hand, the life principle reduces edema and congestion and gives you a new skin, tissue and cells. Life is a self-healer. It forgives and heals. Life holds no grudges against you, and it always keeps forgiving you.

As it's written in Mark 11:25, "*And when you stand praying, forgive, if you have fought against any. Your mind body and soul start becoming light when you forgive.*"

Forgiveness is moving on and letting go of the past grudges and wounds. Forcing yourself to try to like the person who has hurt you is not what forgiveness means. It is letting it go. Release the heavy burden of anger, leaving the past behind and looking for a bright new day. This is your time, your day; you must move on!

Early in my age, I heard a story about a saint in the congregation:

> *One day a saint was having a bath on the edge of a flooded river. It so happened that because of the flood, a scorpion happened to float by. On seeing the plight of the scorpion, that it might die, the saint picked it up in his hand, but immediately had to go away, for the scorpion gave him a piercing poisonous bite, which hurt.*
>
> *The saint didn't mind the bite and again picked up the scorpion and again the scorpion bit his hand. This*

happened many times. One passerby saw the whole incident and asked the saint why he was trying to help the scorpion if it was continuously hurting him.

The saint replied, "When this poor scorpion, who is not able to save itself, is not able to let go of his habit of biting, then how could a saint let go of his habit of helping and forgiving?"

What a great practitioner of compassion and forgiveness this saint was.

Despite being bitten, he was able to practice forgiveness owing to the feeling of compassion within. This is how forgiveness can be truly defined. A true practitioner of forgiveness never thinks of the results of the acts by the other, but remains concentrated on the end of the spiritual laws.

Forgive, whether the sinner repents or not. Forgiveness is a gift you give to yourself, challenging you to believe that there is a better future and that gives you the inner confidence to know that you will survive the pain and suffering. If you don't heal yourself, you will bleed on people who didn't cut you. Faster healing comes when you can let it go and stop allowing it to fester inside like a volcano ready to erupt.

Forgive others, not because they deserve forgiveness, but because you deserve peace. Without forgiveness, there is no peace.

> *"One who is weak from within can never forgive."*

Forgiveness is the attribute of the strong. In order to forgive, you must understand the other person's state of mind and let god handle it. By leaving everyone's karma to their own is the best way to forgive. *The Law of Karma says, whatsoever a man soweth, that shall he also reap.*

When a bird is alive, it eats ants; when the bird is dead, it's the other way around. Time is very powerful, let karma do it on its own. Remember, revenge will never solve anything, karma will. So, forgive!

Forgiveness lets you regain your personal power. Your anger, regret, hatred, or resentment towards someone means that you are giving up your power to that person. Your thoughts and actions will be affected by them and you will envision a chain around your neck, held by the one who wronged you. Until you forgive, you won't break that chain and the person will still have an unhealthy hold on you and you will not be able to free yourself.

Practicing forgiveness brings a feeling of extreme calm and compassion for mankind in general. The practice of forgiveness normally cannot be practiced by the common man, for it requires practicing patience to its extreme.

Forgiveness helps you to feel light and get rid of hard feelings that occupy your mind and heart and eat away your peace of mind. It is a way to self-fulfillment. People who can readily forgive others are much more responsible and satisfied inside than those who keep grudges against others and develop feelings of enmity. The feeling of anguish only results in arguments, fights, mistreatments and war in certain cases. Those who forgive help create positive energy on this planet.

When you hold resentment toward another, you are bound to that person or condition by an emotional link that is stronger than steel. Forgiveness is the only way to dissolve that link and get free.

I was reading somewhere about the author of a bestseller book *Left to Tell: Discovering God Amidst the Rwandan Holocaust.*

During the Rwandan genocide in the mid-nineties, the entire family of a woman named Immaculle Ilibagiza was murdered in a massacre. Immaculle chose to forgive the people who were behind the death of her family and went on to write the bestselling book titled Left to Tell. *She was the founder of 'Left to Tell' Charitable Fund in order to help children who were rendered orphans due to the genocide.*

Rwanda's history was marred by tragic cultural genocide, yet decades later, healing and reconciliation have begun throughout the country. This is an incredible reminder of the power of forgiveness, to heal not only individuals, but communities.

> *"Inner peace can be reached only when we practice forgiveness. Forgiveness is letting go of the past, and is, therefore, the means for correcting our misperceptions even of past lives."*

When you forgive, you do not only release the other person. You set yourself free from all that agony as well.

One thing to keep in mind is to not just forgive others, but also yourself. By forgiving yourself, you will stop the guilt part of yourself and live a positive life.

> *"Forgiveness is the first step towards peace."*

7

Strength of Love

"Love in itself is the complete highest healing power of the universe."

The greatest strength of the universe is 'love'. Love is the source of all good feelings. Every good feeling unites you with the force of love.

Loving means taking caring and helping others whenever and wherever possible.

Love means helping others at times when they need that help the most.

Love means praying for oneness.

Love means to practice humanity.

Divine and unconditional love

"The absence of judgment and the presence of acceptance is love."

There are two kinds of love – human love and divine love. The difference between the two is that human or personal love is often conditional or limited in nature and mostly depends on need; while divine love is spiritual love also known as "*ishq hakiki*" in Sufism. It is infinite in nature and unconditional.

Often in personal or human love, there are aspects of possessiveness, demand or expectation that are all based on condition, limitation, material, selfish desire and need.

Any relationship you have, or you served, there are three types of expectations:

- Expectation of return.
- Expectation of reward.
- Expectation of reciprocation.

You don't even realize that when you think you are doing things for others' sake, for your love for them, you are still motivated by selfishness. Ponder over it. In all relationships, you are motivated by these three expectations.

Unconditional love should never be confused or misunderstood with sentimental love, the attraction between two people, infatuation, sexual love or lust, love for family or friends, or where the word "love" is used very loosely as a sign of friendship, affection or simply as an expression of endearment.

Unconditional love is best described as a state of energy, vibration, a powerful force of higher frequency, ultimately the very highest expression of energy and vibration of all emanating as it does from the very highest, purest and divine energy of the source.

Divine love is unconditional love. When a soul loves another soul without having expectations and desires, it becomes pure love. The soul's main purpose is to serve another soul. Divine love only grants the happiness to the other soul and vice versa.

Your experience of love is to feel a certain sweetness of emotion of love and happiness. It may be stimulated by a person, but essentially it happens within you. You see it everywhere – flowers are blooming, there is love in the air. It's using other person as a key to open your heart, but if you wake up in the morning and you are overflowing with joy, love and happiness, then you are the love because at that time you don't need any person or an entity to love, the love is in you. You become the source of love. It releases the attachment of need. Whether the person is with you or not, divine love always takes care of others. It pours love from the soul of a person to the soul of another person. The fundamental of need is craving for ego. So, need is totally debarred from the divine love which is a part of human love. Divine love is defined in one word: 'give'.

It's a total acceptance of another soul with all the flaws and errors and without any possessiveness.

Inevitably, unconditional love leads to:

- Closeness to god
- Dignity
- Freedom from worldly attachments
- Spiritual growth (inner growth)
- Contentment (happy hearts and soul)
- Acceptance and forgiveness
- Harmony with the universe
- Independence to achieve own life purpose

- Life full of gratitude
- Self-Responsibility

Unconditional love can be of three types:

1. There is only you
2. There is only me
3. There is only one

There is only you

The love where a person loses his/her own identity, they lose themselves in the love and feel that there is only the other person in them. At that stage, they feel the whole existence of other in their self; when they see themselves in the mirror they feel the other in them. Their souls are so merged in the other that they lose their own identity.

Radha's love for Shri Krishna was like that. Radha lost herself in the love of Krishna. For her, she was Krishna, her entire being becomes Krishna. She didn't need Krishna for her love to be accomplished, she didn't want anything from Krishna. Her love was so deep that her soul could easily feel the divinity of Krishna in her.

Here is an excerpt from *The Hindu:*

> *Once Krishna was seated with his consort Rukmini. Krishna covered himself with a blanket as if he was feeling feverish. Worried, Rukmini asked him what the matter was. Krishna said when he would be in Brindavan, Radha used to give him a cup of milk before he went to bed. Lack of that milk was the reason for his not feeling well.*

Rukmini said she would fetch some milk for Krishna. She went to Radha's house. When she heard that Krishna felt unwell because he had not had his usual glass of milk at bedtime, Radha immediately drank some milk! Rukmini could not understand the reason for Radha's action. Why should Radha drink milk when it was Krishna who needed it? Rukmini went back to Krishna and found that he was using the blanket to cover his feet. She moved the blanket aside and found boils (blisters)on his feet. She was taken aback when she saw the boils for, they had not been there when she had left to meet Radha. What had happened in the interim? Krishna clarified that Radha had drunk very hot milk. He resided in Radha's heart and the hot milk had scalded his feet, and hence the boils on his feet! This incident is proof of Radha's unique place among the gopikas. She drank milk to make the Lord feel better. What further acknowledgement of Radha's unconditional love is needed than this endorsement from the Lord who himself confirmed that he resided in her heart?

There is only me

It's the state of unconditional love, where she feels the beloved to be her; his happiness, his sorrows, his pain, his sadness, his achievements all seems to be hers. She indulges herself in that love so much that even time, space and distance don't matter to her. She can feel his vibrations and aura in spite of being continents apart. She can feel his pain staying apart. There is only she, who resides in him, the telepathy, astral projections and intuitions are the psychic powers that come due to this type of unconditional love.

There is only one
The highest form of unconditional love. It is oneness.

The feeling of oneself, there is neither you nor me, everything is one, the love beyond bodies, love on the soul level. The presence of only now, no past, no future; the love which is beyond the mortal. You can experience the whole universe by this love; all the hidden powers come in front of you by the love which is beyond body, colour or shape. You feel their presence in you and you in them and both of you in everyone and everywhere. Such love is eternal.

In the perspective of manifestation
If you feel good, you give love. If you are feeling happy, you are on a very high frequency of love. If you see a child and feel happy, then surely you love that child. All the good feelings, all the high vibrations, come from love. Love is the greatest power that exists in the universe and is a very crucial part of manifesting each desire in your life.

Whatever you desire, you must want it with all your heart and soul. The wish or a desire is purely a form of love. Until and unless you have a burning desire in your heart, you will not have enough power to harness the force of love. So, you need to have a burning and unshakeable desire, the one which you love the most. It should always be in your subconscious mind. So, you must really desire about your wanting, as a businessman desires for a big business, a dancer wants to dance, and a kid wants a toy. When you start loving your desires, you are advancing towards it with full enthusiasm. Love with an unshakable faith that whomsoever you love will love you back, no matter for how long and when.

Love brings an innate power in the soul of a person. It gives the strength to fight under any circumstances for their beloved. That's why it is termed as power. I'm sharing with you the real-life story about immense love of Rick Hoyt and Dick Hoyt.

To date, the inspirational pair has finished 1,091 events, including 252 triathlons, seventy marathons, ninety-four half marathons and 155 five-kilometer races, and maintain their proud record of never having finished last.

Rick was born with cerebral palsy and is quadriplegic, the result of oxygen deprivation at birth.

During his birth, doctors were blunt. They said, "Forget Rick! Put him in an institution, he's going to be a vegetable for the rest of his life."

Today he is fifty-one years old and we still haven't figured out what kind of vegetable he is. And guess what? That vegetable has been turned into a bronze statue.

The statue that will be unveiled outside Boston's Center Elementary School will honour what the two men have done over a thousand times since the mid-70s as Team Hoyt.

Never even thinking for a second to institutionalize their son, Hoyt's decision to raise him like they were his two other brothers and gave him immense love and care.

They took him camping, cross-country skiing and swimming at the beach and enrolled him into school, where he learned to spell words with his eyes - one at a time.

He graduated from high school and from Boston University and now lives on his own with personal care attendants.

It was while at school he told his father he would like to participate in a five-mile charity run for a Lacrosse player who had been paralyzed in an accident.

Rick came home from that basketball game and he said, "Dad, I have to do something for him. I want to let him know that life goes on even though he's paralyzed. I want to run in the race."

Dick was so touched with this statement; his love was so immense and unconditional for his son. He started practicing running; he agreed to push his son in his wheelchair and they completed the run together.

Later that night, Rick told his father: "Dad, when I'm running, it feels like I'm not handicapped."

That sparked the creation of Team Hoyt, an astonishing feat of love and courage that has seen the father and son compete in more than a thousand races, including marathons, triathlons and Ironman competitions.

During triathlons, Dick pulls his son in a boat from a cord attached to his waist during the swim, the pair rides a special two-seater bicycle for the bike section and Dick pushes Rick in a custom-made running chair for the final stage.

The incredible pair set up the Hoyt Foundation in 1989, which aims to include disabled young Americans into daily life, especially through sports, in school and in the workplace.

In 2009, they completed their thousandth race together at the Boston Marathon.

The two had a special wheelchair designed for them and Dick recalled how people didn't understand what they were trying to do together.

"I used to get letters and phone calls saying, 'What are you doing dragging your son to all these races for? Are you just looking for glory for yourself?' What they didn't realize was that he was dragging me to all these races!"

When he was asked for the one thing he would like to give his father, Rick said: "The thing I'd most like for my dad is to sit in the chair and I would push him for once."

Love: *the book written by Dick Hoyt about his incredible journey with his son and right competing again in 1998.*

Both men now give speeches across the U.S., as well as continue to compete in events together in a bid to encourage other disabled young people to challenge themselves.

They have been competing as a team for more than thirty years, and their website says they have no plans on retiring.

This is the true power of unconditional love.

Remember the silver rule: "Giving love is receiving love". Look for buildings you love, the roads, the people you love, the birds, the trees, the flowers, the person, the kids, the gadgets, the clouds. Love each and everything. See, hear, feel and speak of what you love.

Even after all this time, the sun never says to the earth, "You owe me," and look what happens with a love like that! It lights the whole sky.

It's not how much we give, but how much love we put into giving it that's more important. The feelings, emotions linked to love will take you to achieve whatever you want.

Not only saying, but if you feel like what you say, if you feel the love inside, you will be on your higher vibration and you will achieve whatever you want, because love is the basis of every need. Start loving everyone.

Love has a physiological effect on the body. Have you ever noticed how much better you feel physically and how your mood improves when you receive some loving expression from someone who really loves you? Loving and being loved improves your physical health by boosting the immune system and effectuates the feeling of calmness in the brain that controls the mood outlook on life, and feelings of well-being. That higher feeling of giving and receiving will raise your vibrations and the frequencies. Love is the most powerful frequency to achieve anything in lives, in any field, health – wealth, inner peace and happiness.

Love is the key to secrets;
Love is the key to miracles;
Love is the key to inner peace and contentment;
Love is the greatest strength.
Love is the only solution to every problem.
Love is humanity;
Love is life.

Clarity of mind means clarity of passion too. Therefore a great and clear mind loves ardently and sees distinctly what it loves. The clarity of mind, the burning desire should be very clear and to give love to that burning desire with the magic of gratitude, you can achieve each and everything in your life.

Choose the things you love. When you see your favorite flower, say, "I love this flower, it's so beautiful." When you see your favorite car, say, "Wow! I love this car." Wherever you are, and whatever you do, be in love. True love gives you the strength and courage to manifest your dreams

> *"To open the gates of happiness, one should love fearlessly."*

8

Miracles in Relationships

"Not returning evil for evil or insult for insult, but giving a blessing instead, for you were called for the very purpose that you might inherit a blessing."

–Peter 3:9

The Law of Relationship is to give love; the love with no expectations, no rewards. The force of love in the almighty will convey your love message from one soul to another and will heal their soul too.

If someone utters toxic words about your relationships or insults you or does wrong to you, you just need to wave love to them with the feelings of gratitude and love in your heart. You will see the positive difference without saying and doing anything in a relationship.

Give love to others in the form of gratitude, kindness, and appreciation, through your thoughts, through encouragement, through selfless servings of your body, money, mind and feelings. Send the love waves through your thoughts from the formless almighty to the relationships. As you love yourself, love your closest one.

If you give love, gratitude and appreciation in a relationship, it will come back to you manifolds; and if you give hatred, judgment, criticism and anger, it is guaranteed that it will hit you back, at the same frequency and attract the same frequency. So, the positive mental attitude will definitely attract positivity. As per Newton's third law:

"Every action has equal and opposite reaction."

The divine almighty always responds to the vibrational frequencies of your thoughts. Go on in your life with positive vibrations, and positivity will follow you.

When you love with a pure soul and heart, then time-space is no bar for you. The universe gives you the freedom to go through it and give love to the person you love, which is a form of telepathy.

When you feel some synchronicity in your life, then you are living a life by giving love and you are in connection with this formless divine almighty.

When you are joyful and happy, then you say yes to life and have fun. You start projecting positivity all around you and become the sun who sits in the centre of every constellation. People will want to be around you and they will enjoy your company.

The first thing to do when you feel that there is room for more love in your life is to fill your thoughts and actions with nothing but love. By flooding your mind with the feeling of positivity and love for yourself and those around you, your ability to love and be loved back will shine through others.

Gratitude is another crucial aspect of manifestation of love, which can be the key to unlock the abundance of love that is waiting to bring glorious color into your world.

Be grateful for all the love that you are blessed with in life, no matter how much it may be. It is a sure way of recovering abundance of love into your life from the universe, love from a partner, love from the things you enjoy, love from other. Being thankful for so much love will surely result in one thing – that is love and a lot more love!

Have a grateful feeling for each task performed by you. If you feel thankful in your heart, you will win.

If you think and feel that you will never find love, then the universe will bring you more instances where you will find love.

Don't Look at your relationships as it is now, but visualize it, draw a picture of it in your mind, love that picture day and night. You will get what you want.

Firstly, focus on loving yourself.

Loving yourself is accepting yourself fully.

To feel beautiful means to be yourself and your uniqueness is your best quality. You don't need to be accepted by others, you need to accept yourself.

Focus on how wonderful you are. Just focus on one thing that is good about you, keep focusing on it and the formless almighty will give you more things that you will like about yourself.

If you love and accept yourself, it directly affects the quality of your relationships, your work, your free time, your faith and your future.

Don't be at the mercy of your emotions. Use them, make them your power and enjoy them in your life.

Relationships are the mirror of yourself. If you love yourself, you love others. If you hate yourself, you hate others. In relationships with others, it is only you, who is in every relation. You reflect your light, your love or your hatred.

Feeling worthy requires you to see yourself with fresh eyes of self-awareness, love and acceptance. The love must come from within. You don't have to be different to be worthy; your worth is in your true nature, your love and inner goodness. You are a beautiful light, you are love. You can bury your magnificence but not destroy it.

You are a precious and beloved child of god. Read it with reassurance, as per Luke 15:31, "*You are always with me and all that is mine is yours.*"

You should be as positive as you can. When you feel like you are the happiest person in the universe, then you are on the right frequency. Remember, positivity, happiness and love can attract people, animals and even angels. When you give love in relationships, you will get it back. You are giving them the frequencies of love, care and appreciation and they will also feel the same for you.

Sharing a situation when I was struggling with a rude boss:

> *My boss used to shout at me and insult me often. The good thing was that I never got tensed. I just prayed for him to the almighty – to grant him calm and a peaceful mind. I felt that there must be some pressure in his mind; that's why he was giving pressure to me. I adopted a way to cope with the problem.*

When I used to come home, I would spend five minutes to write five good qualities of my boss and I did it every day. I found five good qualities and five ways he helped me. I thanked him in my mind and felt gratified. The behaviour of my boss changed. In fact, he felt sorry for his misbehaviour. Time passed and that boss started praising me in front of higher officials and people. As time changed his behaviour, my positive frequencies changed his negative frequencies.

It's the best way. Whenever you feel some problematic situation in any relation, just say, "Thank you," for anything they had ever done to you. You will see the difference.

The eternal law about relationship is that hate is not conquered by hate. Hate is conquered by love. Learn to fall in love with yourself fully and truly. The more you learn to love and accept yourself, the more you learn to recognize other people's love too. Begin by loving yourself, accepting yourself, just the way you are. Work on accepting your weaknesses, your strengths, your limitations, your guilt and insecurities as a part of your daily routine. You can be happy now. By doing this work, you are recreating your world and embracing your capacity to love.

The second step is letting go

If you want to design your future effectively, you must first let go of your past. It's mandatory.

Holding on to the past is the worst thing you do in relationships. Holding on to grudges will spoil your positive attitude and your relationships, I have already discussed about forgiveness.

Letting go of your past will clear your heart chakra and will make you acceptable for love and care.

The first step in letting go the past is to determine your reason for wanting to let go the past. Ask yourself, "What are the reasons that you must move beyond this? How will your life change? How will it change the trajectory of your relationships? How will you feel in this new chapter of your life where the past life grudges are not there?"

By letting go, you can easily conquer fear. When you leave something behind and don't know what to replace it with, you leave a space for something unknown. Change is always scary, especially when you don't know what is coming next. That's why you might find yourself clinging to the unwanted because that's what is familiar and known to you.

Know your desires to experience a thing, but don't hold on out of fear of doubt. The more you cling to the need of wanting, the more disastrous your manifesting will be.

Allow yourself to feel fully contended and confident. Those who understand how the universe and these vibrations work, understand the power of intention and don't feel stressed or needy. You know that the formless almighty is working for you, and what you create will soon manifest. You create and let go and then you move into the state of receiving.

There is a great paradox that comes with letting go, because a very large part of manifestation requires that you give a lot of focus to your desire; but there is a delicate balancing act of focus without feeling needy.

When you let go of what you are then, you come into the state of receiving any negative feeling. You become worthy and allow yourself to receive the result.

Being human comes with the risk of being wounded. Whether we have experienced a difficult childhood or were rejected or abused in a relationship, the fact is that deep down at the level of heart, we all have emotional wounds that need healing. The preparation for welcoming the loving relationship requires to make a conscious commitment to start healing the deepest wounds of your heart. Notice that I said "start" healing the deepest wounds of your heart, because for most people, this is a lifelong process and it doesn't mean you have to be fully healed to manifest one.

Be like a tree, let the dead leaves drop and don't feel the pain at the separation of dead leaves. The one who comes will go someday.

A good relationship heals the deepest of wounds, but you must be willing to clear out all the past pains, bruises, resentments and anything else that makes up the thick walls of protection and distrust around your heart. So, your responsibility should start at this very moment, to gently uncover the wounds of your heart and begin the healing process so that you can send out a clear signal to the formless almighty that you are being healed and now ready to love and start doing it right now.

Accept fully where you are, embrace it completely. Say yes to all worries, shame and guilt. Confirm all the negative thoughts and feelings so that you can release yourself from their grip. Just give up the battle and stop judging.

The third step in relationships is to stop judging

Judgments often come from the misunderstanding that others do not see or experience the world like you do. You have had a different childhood and experiences and you saw the world through your own unique spectacle.

When you find yourself unintentionally judging your partner, you may notice that you don't feel as close or connected to him/her as you were before. This is because judging creates separation.

Love is neither a measurement, nor a judgment. Love is about who helps you grow and expand your personality.

No one is perfect, everyone has their own flaws, but all are unique creatures of the formless lord.

Judgment is a game of conflict, so it diminishes the understanding level of one another to a negligible state.

Many of us believe that love comes from sacrificing, tolerating, suffering or silence, but that's not true. Love comes from devoting ourselves to our beloved, not in the want of being loved back, but with an unshakable faith. That way, the resultant gratification is one of a true kind.

The secret to experience deeper love is allowing each other to grow. Yes, allowing each other to live their own life fully, to grow and nourish.

The 3 a's of relationship

- Acceptance
- Appreciation
- Attention

Acceptance

Acceptance is what will get you through to the other side. Some people don't know the meaning of acceptance; they just learned that in relationships, defending and withholding will improve the relationship. They are always on the lookout to fend off criticism or a correction. They need them to be perfect. They don't realize that in changing a person beyond their personal limits will make them lose the person. Acceptance doesn't mean resignation; it means understanding that something is what it is and that you can choose it for exactly what it is.

Once there is acceptance, you bring peace and change to your energy. From there, anything you create with the person you love is possible.

Acceptance is loving the person as it is. Whatever they are, just say you are with them, under any circumstances. Your total support will nourish their soul and make you and them the happiest and loving souls, because when you choose it for what it is and what it isn't, it brings something entirely new into your world. When you reach the point where you and your relative can accept each other fully, the very quality of your experience changes entirely. Your relationship will be transformed. Celebrate the differences in you, accept them and embrace them.

> *I was very talkative, jolly and a happy person. I saw people through souls. In some family gatherings and parties, I spoke freely and laughed loudly without thinking that I am a daughter-in-law of the family. As in rural India, these things mean a lot to the families. My loud talks always irritated my family. Although I*

was also from the same social circle, my inner world was something different and connected to the universe through deep meditations from an early age of my life. I loved nature, enjoyed all happy moments, but the perception of my family was not like that. They told me to talk slowly, and I changed myself and stopped speaking. I was not balanced; either I could talk freely or I could stop talking. I changed myself, but the inner me was dead, destroyed and it was something which wanted to breathe.

It was my husband Rajeev Chawla who accepted me as I was. He encouraged me to fly high, do whatever I wanted in my life, and be happy., His total acceptance made me learn the things my family wanted to convey – to be balanced, to get saved from any betrayals,

"His acceptance gives me wings to fly, and feet to dance and the love to adore."

Even now, in parties and family gatherings, we dance fiercely, laugh loudly and love unconditionally. We both accept each other's differences and still love each other with a lot of respect for each other.

That's not to say that you must accept everything in your relationship. You shouldn't accept any abuse, physically or emotionally. You should have similar core values and a vision for your future.

1. You must accept those things in a relationship, which you can't change.
2. You must accept that no one is perfect. Love is to accept imperfection.
3. You must accept that everyone is raised differently, have their life experiences and also past life pains. So, everyone's perception of life is different. That's why, embrace the differences.
4. You must accept that they are also human and they make mistakes. It's okay, we also make mistakes.
5. You must accept that everyone has a past. It's not only their journey, but it's their souls' journey too. Whatever is meant to be, will definitely happen, but you must accept their past.
6. You must accept their errors and flaws which you can't change.
7. You must accept that just because they don't behave like you, they are not wrong.
8. You must accept them fully, with respect.

Celebrate the differences. Sometimes you even have to agree to disagree, but that does not change your love for the other person. It is your differences that make for interesting conversations. It is your differences that increase your perspective of the world, if you are willing to truly listen. It is your differences that make your relation unique and exciting.

> *"Acceptance of others, their looks, their behaviours, their beliefs their perceptions, bring you an inner peace and tranquility – instead of anger, anxiety, and resentment."*

When you accept that you are feeding your vibrational energy into resisting something, you make a problem more powerful and sticky in your subconscious mind. Instead, somewhat counter intuitively, when you accept what it is, it loses much of its power. There is so much you can affect. What you cannot change, what you cannot influence, no matter what, should not be a concern to you.

And now when you accept things, people, as they are, you will be free from your mind and soul. You will become light as a feather, as you won't have any grudges and anger in your mind. You would feel stillness inside. Now, accepting doesn't mean giving up. It just means that you put yourself in a better position to take action, if necessary, but don't worry about it. Because now you can see more clearly, you can focus your vibrational frequency towards what you want and take the appropriate action to change your situation.

Appreciation

> *"The deepest principle of human nature is a craving to be appreciated."*

Appreciation is a key to any relationship. Appreciating someone makes them feel good about what they do, and that makes a difference to their lives. They will feel good and joyful. It makes them feel better about themselves, urging them to go on with a new vigour and strengthening your relationship. Once you learn how to accept a relationship, you can then move on to appreciation. Your priorities shift with time and changing the person is way less important than loving them for who they are. From this place of acceptance, you shift to appreciation. If you take time, you might even see that their irritating behaviour may even have value. It's important for them to know that they have made a difference in your life.

> *"Appreciation is a beautiful gift, which we give to someone and ourself simultaneously."*

When you appreciate them, they feel privileged and more energetic to do more for you, to do more which is being appreciated. Appreciation is an acknowledgment of their love and deeds. When you give them a sincere compliment or words of encouragement, you are making their world a better place. You are making them feel appreciated and valuable. Any approval for something they have done will not only enhance their lives, you will enrich yours. You will feel more fulfilled because you have done something to make their life better. It will accelerate the relationship building process and enhance their overall impression of you. What you give, you get in return.

When I was a kid, my father appreciated me on making chapatis, although I knew that those chapattis were not round and appropriate to eat, but it increased my confidence and trust. It was a total acceptance of my father for me, and then I practiced daily to serve the best food and the same thing happened with my daughter. Now, my daughter, in spite of a non-working right hand can make wonderful food, leaving behind many professional chefs.

That's how appreciation creates a bond between you and the person you appreciate. It initiates a zeal to work more for others. But remember, appreciation should not be a lie; it will be caught immediately.

Once I woke up and came out of the washroom, my hair messy. I was feeling so sleepy and there was not even a single sign of smile on my face. Suddenly, my husband shouted, "Oh my god! Sargam, you are looking gorgeous..." and we both started laughing. (We had discussed this whole concept of appreciating each other a day before.) He wanted to appreciate me and wanted me to feel good, but I knew that I was not looking gorgeous at that time. So, lies will immediately be caught, but still leave smiles on the faces.

Some simple ways to appreciate:

1. Saying thank you and acknowledging the little things they do every day.
2. Show them the reasons why you are grateful to them and give specific examples.
3. When they help you out, give them a hug or a kiss, or a pat on their back. Physical touch is a powerful technique to give love and appreciation.
4. Appreciate little things, like if they give you a glass of water, or bring some fruits or groceries from the market, appreciate them. Thanking them for little things makes a big difference.
5. Appreciate anything that adds value to your relationship and tell them about it regularly.

6. Appreciate them for being there with you through your ups and downs; they are investing their precious time.
7. Appreciate them when they wear a new dress, tell them it suits them, the colour suits them. It will boost up their confidence and joy.
8. Healthy relationships are the ones that keep evolving. When it comes to love, appreciating someone is never enough. Give acceptance, appreciation and love.

Attention

Attention in a relationship is noticing, listening, watching and taking care of your close ones. Usually people take their loved ones for granted; they forgot to pay attention to the little things. Sometimes in the family, they sit in the same room but are busy with their mobiles, laptop or TV screens. Relationships require attention, every day and every time.

Attention is to take care of the little unnoticed things in our relationships. You should know the likes and dislikes of the other person.

With the responsibilities of being an adult in a fast-paced world, it can be hard to stop, talk, and listen. Communication is the heart of a successful relationship, though. Without it, it is easy to lose touch.

Paying attention to each other allows the relationship to grow and improves intimacy.

If a woman or man is complaining to you, remember that it means they trust you enough to express their feelings. Don't betray that trust.

There are many ways to pay attention:

1. At least once in a day, you must say "I love you"; express your love and gratitude towards them.
2. Keep track of the little things. It includes paying attention to small details and doing special things that we know each other will like. Being thoughtful helps you to live, connect and to love more deeply.
3. Treat them as a celebrity when they come home after work, it will make them feel like a king or a queen.
4. Pay attention to their normal health problems, as when they are not feeling well, instantly take decision about their food and consultations, if necessary.
5. Be attentive, when they want to discuss their stress level and its cause. Listen to them. Listening is more than just hearing. It's paying attention to body language, head nodding, asking questions, and showing you are engaged in the conversation. Sometimes, just taking the time to genuinely listen to what they have to say, and not saying anything at all, will say more to them than your words ever could.
6. Notice them; appreciate them, when they look good. Little ways of noticing will increase your interaction with each other.
7. Talk about your feelings, frustrations, or ambitions on that particular day. Discuss about the day events and people's behaviour.
8. Just make a conscious effort to put your phone away whenever you are giving your attention. Putting your phone away sends the message that you are there in the moment.

9. The more time you spend together, the more chances you have to be attentive, to show interest, to be affectionate, and to get to know your relation even better.

"Love is not written on a paper, for a paper can be erased. Love is not etched on a stone, for a stone can be broken. Love is inscribed on a heart, and there it shall remain forever."

–Rumi

9

Manifesting the Abundance of Health

"Whatever diseases we have in our bodies, the natural forces within us know how to heal."

What is a good health? The person who is able to dance like a child, or jump like a child, a person who has no burden in his mind. A person who can stand instantly and immediately as a child and sit instantly and immediately like a frog. How active is that person? He, who has the same attributes as written above, is definitely a healthy person.

When the point of health is being discussed, everyone is definitely concerned with the healing of body organs, mental and other physical affairs.

No mental or religious science practitioners, psychologists, psychiatrists or medical doctors can heal a patient until the patient himself wants to be healed.

The immense power of the universe and the almighty heals everything. As it is the law of the universe, the trees or the animals don't see doctors or any type of religious mentors who help them to heal. If you see closely, the law of nature grows a tree from a seed. Growth and healing is a law in itself.

I was driving my car; suddenly I saw a log of wood that was a part of the big tree which was being cut down. I saw small stems shooting out of that log, which would grow as shoots after some days. I smiled and realized how nature had healed a big tree which was cut down by humans. A tree which had no leaves to make food, but still, it was healing itself and coming to life again. It had retained its charm and beauty by only being attached with the soil. How amazing it was! What healing!

Nature and the almighty have the immense power to heal anything. Again it's the process of vibrational frequency, your connection with the universe through your positive thoughts and the faith that heals you as soon as possible.

All diseases originate in the mind of a human; nothing can appear on the body unless there is a mental pattern corresponding to it. The power of your thoughts is the cause of disease and also the cause of healing.

My grandfather was eighty-six years old. He got a paralysis attack and the doctor placed a catheter (urine pipe) and a colostomy bag. He was not able to go to the congregation (religious meet) as he felt ashamed, which made him too upset. Three days after he got the attack, he started immense prayers and forced the doctor to remove the colostomy bag. The doctor and the whole family insisted him not to do that, but he didn't listen to anyone. His faith in the almighty was so deep that he acted as a stubborn child and the doctor had to remove it. But after that, he didn't have any problem. He was healthy and the doctor was literally shocked.

What was it that made an old man take a stand? Actually, that was his unshakeable faith. Pay attention on how inner thoughts, your willpower, and your immense faith make impossible things to become possible and your belief system can heal you immediately.

Much about a person's health can be determined by the frequency of the person's body. If the body's frequency is high, the person is healthy and happy.

A lady named "KOMAL" is a member of our Nirankari congregation. She had breast cancer, but she was using the universal powers so much that despite having painful chemotherapy treatment in India, I saw her still being regular in the congregation. In the morning, she would go for chemotherapy and in the evening she would come into the congregation to remember the almighty. She was always thankful for her life. From last year, I saw a *drastic improvement in her health and now she is completely free from cancerous cells.*

Again, what was the power behind her that fought against the stubborn cancerous cells?

What was the strength behind the recovery?

What did she do to overcome cancer?

The answer for all these questions is faith.

When unconditional faith accompanies gratitude, it gives you the power; just as Komal made herself powerful enough to fight cancer and won. Due to immense faith, her willpower increased and she became stronger to survive through that tough circumstance.

As it's written in Exodus 15:26: *if you will diligently listen to the voice of the lord, your god, and do that which is right in his eyes, and give ear to his commandments and keep all his statutes, I will put none of the diseases on you that I put on the Egyptians for I am the lord, your healer.*

No disease can ever touch you if you believe in god with complete faith. The whole universe will conspire with you to heal you and to make sure you flousrish.

A cheerful heart is the best medicine for anything, but a crushed spirit and crushed soul dry up the bones of the survivor.

So, a cheerful heart full of happiness with a positive mindset is all about it. You have to smile often, feel like you are dancing, you are on the seventh sky, and subsequently, it affects each cell of your body. Your body starts improving and nourishing.

If you have a health problem, start feeling like you are recovering from that problem, feel like your cells are charging and energy is flowing into each cell of your body. If you feel bad for your body, just go to sleep or go for a long drive, go to the park and feel the beauty of nature. You will definitely recover; in fact, you are already recovered because the supreme soul is with you. He is your shadow. He will take you in his arms and in his lap where he taps you to have a good sleep so as to heal you and you will feel like your cells are recovering from that disease and the ill substance going out of your body. You start feeling as if illness has gone and now you are refreshed, healthier and happier.

Stand up and go for a walk, talk to your family members or your friends, watch nature's beauty (start watching flowers, start watching the sky). You will feel like everything is healing you, say thanks to the Almighty. It is due to him that you are able to stand again.

Yes! You are already healing yourself because you know that it's the law of the universe.

> *"Healing is universal nature."*

Your emotions affect every cell of your body; mind and soul, mental and physical are intertwined. It is said that concentrate on your mind and your thoughts, then you will see the physical disease symptoms starting to vanish.

The biggest experience of my life I have ever shared is the recovery of genetic mutation and that really creates a health miracle.

My daughter was born on 27 February 2004. In the month of October 2004, she fell down from the bed and got a paralysis stroke that hit the right side of her body. It was her right leg and arm.

According to doctors, she had "genetic mutation" and "mitochondrial disorder". A person who is familiar with the science knows that genetic mutation is not a curable illness. I told my husband that the reports said that our daughter would not recover and there was a very less chance of her survival due to lot of infarcts and calcification in her brain. Though it was known in the medical field, that there is a lot of probability that a child might be genetically mutated.

One month later, we went to an annual congregation in Delhi. I met my uncle, who is also a doctor and discussed the problem with him. And what he said changed my entire life. He said; "Sargam! There are millions and trillions of cells in the human body and they are very small to be seen with naked eyes and in these millions of cells there is a nucleus in every single cell, Which is further difficult to see and in that small nucleus there are DNA and in DNA there are hundreds and thousands of genes and those genes are very negligible to see. Although, with the help of very strong microscopes we are able to see the genes. Now, Shudhita (my daughter) has the problem in her genes. It is said that god is omnipotent, omniscient and omnipresent so, it's evident that god is present in each and every grain of the soil. It make us believe in the concept of 'sukshm ' (negligibly small). To believe he is even smaller than the genes, that he is the cause of the problem and he sits deep rooted within the genes, so he will heal the illness as well? Just have faith that the almighty will take care of it and he has already done it."

When I understood the concept of 'sukshm', I left everything to god. I left on the basis of an unshakable faith that my daughter would be cured. In the year 2013 I went for her checkups again to see that if she was still genetically mutated. To my great disbelief, reports were normal. Doctors who were going through regular checkups were alleging supervising doctors.

Actually, the power of faith, the power the universe can manifest anything in our lives.

Affirmations help to reprogram old thought processes to create new patterns, suggests Melissa Carver, PhD.

Use some health affirmations or mantras to keep you on a healthy mode:

"I am ready to enjoy perfect health."

"I am fully capable of healing my body. I know I am recovering."

"I am a special and unique child of this universe, so is my body."

"I am healthy and whole. My body is being healed right now."

"I am full of energy and vitality; all the cells of my body take daily bath in the showers of my divine being."

"My sleep is relaxing and refreshing and heals me every night."

"My mind is in peace and harmony; I enjoy exercising and love healthy food."

"I will relax now, to communicate with my body and my source."

"My only work is to relax and breathe. I can do that and I can do that very easily."

"I have a perfectly healthy body, mind and spirit."

"Daily visualization of the perfect image of every organ creates a shell around you against any disease."

It is easy to reduce weight

The reason you want every single thing you want is that you think you'll feel really good when you get there. But, if you don't really feel good on your way there, you can't get there. You have to be satisfied with what-is while reaching for more."

–Abraham Hicks

What do you see, when you look into the mirror?

Are you happy with what you see?

Your answers have a lot to do with how successfully you can apply the law for weight loss.

"Your thoughts shape your body."

You reach where you are by focusing your thoughts, emotions and actions in a certain direction. You get what you focus on. You make mistakes when you focus on the wrong things. See, when you focus on something, you cannot focus away from that thing.

You cannot focus on "not being overweight", that's the same thing like focusing on being overweight.

See the difference: negation is also an attraction. The universe doesn't like negative sentences. Accept that you are overweight. Mother Teresa knew that, that's why she called for a peace rally and detested the anti-war rally. She always said that she would never attend an anti-war rally, but if they were going to have a peace rally, they may invite her.

Weight gain begins with a single negative thought. A single negative thought that you possess will create more and more negative thoughts until excess of weight has been manifested. Excess weight is the result of negative thinking. It only takes a negative thought to begin it all. No matter what weight you have manifested, a single positive thought can change the whole.

When I got married, everyone in my family used to say that I am very fat. I felt so bad about my body and started hating myself. I tried a lot, like exercising, medicines, dieting, etc., but my weight did not reduce and I was constantly feeling negative. One day in my room, sitting calmly, I prayed to the almighty for manifesting the weight I wanted to put off. I conveyed that I have tried my best and now you (almighty) have to do it. I don't know how you will do it, but it is my burning desire. This practice of stubbornly asking a wish to be granted is also known as hath yoga in spirituality.

The trust and faith on the formless almighty made me feel good and positive. I started ignoring everyone's abuse on my fat body. I started loving my body. It brought a positive change in me and I became more confident. Suddenly, I noticed the reduction in my weight, despite of eating regular food and no more stressful exercises. It made my faith stronger and I became more positive.

Excess weight is a sign that you do not love yourself and are not grateful. Love and gratitude are very important in our lives. They can eliminate all the negativity from our lives. They can help you to reduce weight overnight, melt inches from your body and transform it.

The foundation of all self-care and permanent change is self-love and self-acceptance. The most courageous and powerful decision you can make, is to decide to love yourself and be happy in the present moment. All that you are seeking will come from this.

What you need to do first is to cut out the things that make you feel bad about yourself. Stop looking at other people and constantly comparing yourself to them. If someone is cruel to you, don't spend much time around them and definitely don't waste your time listening to them. Most importantly, stop criticizing yourself.

There are some steps you can follow:

1. State what you want. Say it out loud to yourself or write down and describe it in detail and state how it will make you feel to achieve this goal.
2. If you find a picture of the body that you desire, cut it out and display it in a place where you will see it daily or you can create a vision board with pictures of what you desire and feel good when you look at it. The key is that when you see this picture, imagine it as your own body. You can cut out a picture of the person with your desired body if it will make it easier to visualize it as your own.
3. Whatever you eat, say "thank you" to the formless almighty that food is giving me strength and also making me thin and doing the work for making me slimmer.
4. Express gratitude daily for the delicious food you eat and for the super powerful "water" which can boost up digestion and help you loose weight.
5. Believe that what you want is already yours and stay focused on what you desire, and not on what you currently see. What you want, will come into existence and become reality.

Sometimes people find themselves trapped in a vicious spiral of eating and feeling bad.

All the time you are being shown pictures of the way you should be, all the people surrounding you always comment on your fitness. So you naturally compare yourself and wonder why you don't measure up. This can make you feel bad for yourself; whatever the cause may be. The first force that comes out is 'feeling bad about yourself.' For most of the people, food is a kind of treat, they eat what they love, and whenever they go to a party, they eat snacks and treats and make their mind peaceful. It's an immediate gratifying sensation. The second force that comes out is the 'wrong solution'.

So, you end up spinning round and round between these two different forces, feeling bad about yourself and eating in order to feel better.

It will be of no use, the first and last step is to feel good for yourself, always and whatever life throws on you, just catch it and play with it. Say "thank you" and enjoy.

You will definitely see positive results!!!

10

Becoming a Money Magnet

"When you realize there is nothing lacking, the whole world belongs to you."

Money is a spiritual tool that fuels your soul's ability to have a full experience within its physical plane. Money is nothing more than a form of energy exchange that exists in itself. You choose to engage in this energy exchange every time you go to the confectionery shop to buy the things you need to survive.

You have chosen to come here and incarnate into a physical being and experience your life.

Now, you are consciously aware that it is your choice to use money as a form of energy exchange within your life experience, you can decide consciously what money really means to you and it matters.

The universe is abundant; it has enough resources to fulfill everyone's needs and wishes. The universe knows the shortest possible path to fulfill your dreams, which is a miracle in itself.

Anyone who lives within their means, suffers from a lack of imagination; you need to dream big to achieve big.

Yes, all your wishes, all your dreams can come true, when you are ready to manifest it. In the previous chapters we have already discussed how to demand from the formless almighty. Share your burning desires with the almighty in your prayers.

When you dream, you feel good and you achieve higher vibrations, and then the Almighty starts his work to fulfill your dreams.

It's the attractive force of love and gratitude towards wealth that moves all the money in the world and whosoever is giving love by feeling good is a magnet for money.

Love is the greatest power of the universe. Whatever the thing is, whatever the wish is, whatever the dream is, the only reply to every question – the solution to every problem is love, love and love.

The simple rule is to love money! After all, it's just energy and energy flows freely. This principle is the reason why you can manifest money at will. Simply by putting out an intention and following your inner guidance.

Your intention is like a little seed. It needs to be nurtured so that it can sprout and grow. Therefore, you need to give it energy through spirituality.

The more love you give to your intention, the more energized it becomes. Use creative ways to help you hold your love to your intention by writing it down, posting it on the wall, reciting it aloud, memorizing or sharing your dream with close ones. Manifest love in each and every action of yours.

Pay attention to how you feel and think. Your intentions and your attitude determine if this theory will work on you or not. Letting go of resistance and negative thoughts are also key elements to know how the theory practically operates on you.

Money will come to serve those who love everyone, who love the entire universe; the trees, the flowers, the butterflies, the animals, the rain, the sunshine and each and everything that is created by the formless.

All you have to do is to make a list of why you love money.

> *"Money will come to serve those who love the entire creation of the creator."*

As "I love money because it helps me to pay my bills."

"I love money because it helps me to travel the world and I love to travel."

"I love money because it helps me to do good to others in the world."

"I love money because it smells good."

"I love money because I can help others with it."

"I love money because I love to shop."

You need to see yourself as having manifested money today. Your entire vision needs to be that it has already happened. Forget what you see going on in the world around you.

These are some tasks, which are capable of changing the old perceptions of the subconscious mind and creating wonders in manifesting money:

Star gazing

Look at the sky and see the stars. Use your creative visualization skills and go beyond the stars for a minute. Go deeper and wider and allow yourself to realize that you live in a vast and abundant universe that is greater than any tiny wish that you have. Realize that there are endless unused possibilities in the universe.

Feel the vastness of the sky and abundance of the stars.

Talk with money

A great philosopher once said, "Money can't talk, but it can hear." Talk to money and say thank you to the currency you have in your hand. Call wealth into your life on a daily basis using positive affirmations. Just as plants grow and bloom with positive affirmations, so will your bank account when you start speaking to your money. Declare that you are a money magnet and you are receiving all the wealth that is meant for you now.

Sow to grow

Yes, you have to sow before you get what you want.

Money can be sown in many ways, like power of compounding. But in the spiritual context, money can be sown by giving and by charity. The more you give, the more you receive. Sowing your money in the fields of the universe with a positive mental attitude that it will come back in manifolds, will definitely work.

Make space

My colleague, Pooja Chaudhary, cleans her purse daily; she throws the garbage from it and very nicely arranges the currency in her purse.

Cleaning the garbage and making space for what you want is the important part of manifestation. It's a clear indication that you are ready to receive.

In 2012, I was trying my best from the last three years to clear my exam of a government job. I knew only one year was left as it was the last year of my eligibility. When I appeared for the exam one last time, I prayed to the almighty that I need this job and I need my appointment to be in this city only; otherwise my family balance would be disturbed. I also prayed that, god! Time is less and I don't know how to achieve my dream. I just know one thing, that I did my best. It was my burning desire. I prepared for the exam very rigorously and visualized that I have passed the examination.

As already written: "Teri taakat ko yeh dil maan to leta hai magar, har taraf se jab koi raah sujhaayi na pade."

Which means, we only trust on your power, O lord, when there is no solution anywhere. It is only then that we choose to surrender and believe.

I surrendered and I got a letter on March 2013, which was my joining letter for my bank job.

The miracle was that they placed the eligibility of the age of below thirty as on 1 January, although the time of joining was of 30 April 2013 and I would have been above thirty years.

This is how burning desire accompanied with faith, positive attitude and surrender, creates miracles.

Grateful for whatever you have

Gratitude is a "*brahmastra*". It is a "*sanjeevani buti*".

Gratitude is a stepping stone for every success and for every dream to come true.

Giving thanks and appreciating each and everything in your life is an art. Yes, thanksgiving is an art of living.

Make a list of things from your childhood which have not been bought by money but gifted to you by someone else, whether it was from parents, siblings or any other person. Remember all the things from your baby clothes, nappies, baby oil, baby powder, cereals, food, shelter, clothes, studies, enjoyment, toys, luxuries, to your smallest needs which were gifted to you by someone.

Say, "thank you" to them for this. Feel really grateful to them for the same. These were the things you needed and the lord provided it at that time. Say thank you to the almighty for everything he has given you.

Look back into your past. Many people gave you gifts at their expense for your happiness; acknowledge them with a feeling of gratefulness and be thankful in your heart.

Now turn to the things you can't buy using money: love of your parents, the deep love of your mother, the care and love of your father which can't be bought by any wealth. Be grateful for the immense love of your parents.

Be grateful for your health. I am sharing a recent accident:

I got an injury due to which my elbow was crushed and broken into six pieces. The doctors joined each piece with the help of artificial plates and screws were inserted in my arm. Now, doctors asked me to open my fingers and close them. I felt that I was not able to close my fingers. I tried the same procedure on my left hand, and I could close and open the fist. Then, I realized that how beautifully the almighty makes our body, how accurately everything works. And how we take our body parts for granted. So, be grateful for each and every movement of your body. Be grateful for every healthy and working body part which we can't get by spending lots of money and wealth.

See your smile, how beautiful it is. The tears when you are at the happiest state. The time spent with nature. The beach, the garden, the river shore, the rainbow, the flowers, all these things are not conducted and nurtured with money but give us happiness. So, be grateful for all these things.

Gratitude unlocks the fullness of life

It suggests that you have enough and more. It turns denial into acceptance, chaos into order and confusion into clarity. It can turn a simple meal into a feast, a house into a home, a stranger into a friend. It has the power to create a miracle.

"The greatest manifest of wealth is: charity."

"The art of giving is a trait of the rich. It's not he who has much who is rich, but he who gives more is the richest."

Charity is an art of giving. Charity is absolutely and totally essential if we ever want to be truly prosperous. Bear in mind that charity is more about the act and process of giving, and not the thing that has already been given. The energy always flows. So when you give your money, it comes into flow and gets back to you from any other source. Now have a look at thoughts like these in your mind:

"I need money for my family,"

"I have so many needs,"

"Money does not grow on trees," etc.

All of these thoughts will limit your belief system. This type of thinking ensures that there will be a limited supply of money, as the current of the flow of money flows around the pocket of a stagnated thought and stagnated money.

If we keep the money in circulation, then there will always be more than enough for everyone to have what they want and need in life. Charity is not only giving, it's putting your heart and feelings in giving, thanking the almighty for having such resources that you are able to do charity.

> *"No one has ever become poor by giving."*

One of my friends shared this story with me:

One famous scholar, Mr Rakesh, related that his father wanted to see his old friend who was a poor and needy man. He tried to find out his friend and asked people about him. People told him, the person about whom you are talking, was no longer a poor man; he was now a rich person. His father decided to pay a visit to his friend.

While conversing with his friend, he asked him the reason for the change in his economic position. The man replied that he had been very poor to the extent that he was forced, to sell household things that belonged to him, like furniture, etc. By selling these things, he had collected money enough to start a business with.

As he was on his way back to his house with the capital, he saw a poor lady crying. The man asked the lady the reason for crying, and she explained that she was a widow with orphans who were hungry. The man felt pity for her, and on seeing that she needed the money more than him, he gave the whole amount of money to her. He returned home and spent the night depressed and worried for his family.

The next morning, surprisingly, he was summoned to the house of a rich man. When he went to the rich man he was told that he had six thousand bags of wheat which he feared were on the verge of expiring. The rich man suggested him to buy the wheat at a low price on loan from him. The poor man did so and sold the wheat bags quickly. He took some more and in this way was able to make much profit. Soon, he became rich and well to do.

Indeed, the Qur'an says that:

> *"The person who lends to Allah, a good lending will receive many times more."*

The personal sacrifice of giving one's possessions, no matter how small, for the sake of helping those in needs is a blessing and means purifying our souls and wealth. Lapin states, *"Philanthropy is necessary for creating wealth, just as sunshine is for growing flowers."* Charity makes you feel like a better person, which makes you come across many better persons. Giving regular gifts from your income to charity is one excellent way, once and for all, persuading your subconscious that you deserve what lies ahead.

I am very much inspired by my friend, Sarita Juneja, in the field of charity and learned the true meaning of charity from her life. She, although my best friend, never told me about her efforts to save so many homes by giving them regular monthly salary. In fact, the secret was revealed when I asked an old lady how she managed her living as her husband and son both had already passed away. She replied that my friend sent her money every month due to which she was able to live, and gave her lots of blessings. Trust me friends, whatever she asked for, was accomplished every time. Whether it's world tours or luxurious cars or anything she wanted.

Whatever you give with true emotions, will come back to you manifold. Universe is a bank and you are taking out and depositing in your bank account and the interest given by the universe is totally dependent on emotions and faith.

Leave the feeling of jealousy

Jealousy is a negative feeling and the person who feels jealous of someone is at his lowest frequency. When you see someone prosperous and having the same thing you want for yourself in your life, don't feel jealous or sad. In fact, be happy and joyous for them. To overcome this emotion, tell yourself, how wonderful it is, you rejoice in that person's prosperity and achievements. You should wish more success and wealth for that person.

Jealousy is a resistance to your dreams, so be aware of the negative feeling of jealousy. Neutralize your jealousy by truly wishing for him greater wealth in every possible way. It will neutralize the negative thought of your mind and cause an ever greater measure of wealth to flow to you.

Whenever you feel jealous of someone, apologize to the almighty as soon as possible. It will create the positive force of love in your thoughts and you will get rid of the negative feeling.

"If you want to burn your soul, develop jealousy and get destroyed."

Sharing with you the success story of Dr Sanjeev Juneja, magnet of wealth

Dr Juneja, an entrepreneur later, but a best friend and an idol for me first. The man who was little known until he stole the headlines by selling a six-year-old hair care brand (Kesh King), to one of the largest transactions in the country's FMCG sector in recent history.

He sold Kesh King to Emami on 2 June 2015 for Rs 1,651 crores, a valuation that's more than five times its annual sales. The brand notched up Rs 300 crores in sales in year 2014-15, expanding at a compounded annual growth rate of more than 60%.

Dr Juneja was not a well-known businessman with a parental business with him. When he got married, he only had a Vespa scooter to ride and no luxury. He lost his father at an early age, circumstances made him more responsible and caring for his family.

He started his product in 2009, in a setup of a single room. This is what I noticed about his success (in brief):

- Dedication towards his work: *The passion of doing work till late nights, having positive attitude and loved doing what he wanted to do.*
- Burning desire: *The burning desire can't let you sleep. His wife always said that he used to suddenly wake up at night, thinking of his business and used to plan it the whole night.*
- Positivity and gratitude: *He is the most positive person I have ever met. He lives his life to the fullest. The feeling of gratitude is immersed in him for his employees, his family*

members or anyone who crosses his way. He always shows his gratitude towards that almighty, which cause high vibrations and attracts what he wants.

- Strength of Love: *His love for his father and family is so strong and divine that it makes him powerful. The pain of separation from his father and the willingness to maintain happiness of his love inspires him to do and think beyond his limits and belief.*
- Charity: *I have already discussed in this chapter about his wife Mrs Sarita Juneja and her charity, which inspires the universe to help them achieve their dreams and how the giving attract more and more receiving.*

So, this is a small case study of an entrepreneur on how dedication and positive attitude can bring miracles into life.

11

How do Affirmations Work in Manifestations

"The world has enough beautiful mountains and meadows, spectacular skies and serene lakes. It has enough lush forests, flowered fields, and sandy beaches. It has plenty of stars and the promise of a new sunrise and sunset every day. What the world needs more of, are people to appreciate and enjoy it."

–Michael Josephson

Affirmations are statements which are aimed to affect the conscious and the subconscious mind. The words and statements which compose of the affirmation automatically bring up mental images into the subconscious mind which cause visualization and imagination, which could inspire, energize and motivate.

To affirm means to say something positive. It means to declare and have faith in the mind that asserts something to be true. Affirmations are statements where you assert that what you want to be true is true.

Affirmations are easy to do and they don't take much time at all. In just a few minutes, you can change your daily life. Repeating aloud the affirmations will result in giving you the energy you need for the day. By reflecting on your prosperity and abundance, you'll soar above your current highest height. It relieves stress and it creates a space in your subconscious mind to practice gratitude into your daily life. Eventually, it becomes a part of your life.

Repeating affirmations and the resultant mental images affect the subconscious mind by changing the old perspective of thinking, which was the old belief system and which in turn, influences the behaviour, habits, actions and reactions. It means a paradigm shift takes place. An affirmation mostly works because it has the ability to program your mind into believing the stated concept by changing the old perceptions of the subconscious mind. This is because the mind doesn't know the difference between reality and fantasy.

Here are some affirmations:

- I am becoming more and more grateful for what I have in my life.
- I appreciate my life more than ever.
- I love myself; I love my body; I love my soul.
- I feel an abundance of gratitude for everything I have and receive every day.
- The entire universe is a part of the almighty. I do love everyone and everyone loves me back, manifold.

- The almighty pours happiness into my life every day. It has my cup overflowing with wealth, health and unconditional love.
- I am wealthy; I can help anyone with the wealth and money given to me. I am grateful to the almighty for free flowing money into my life.
- I feel gratification for Almighty's endless treasures, which is available to me every time and everywhere.
- I am healthy, my body listens to me. Whatever I command, it reacts instantly, and blood flows freely in my veins.
- I always receive exactly what I ask for, what I think of receiving, the almighty gives me and I appreciate that.
- I am grateful for excellent health, abundance, prosperity and true love.
- My life is filled with an abundance of goodness, an abundance of happiness and an abundance of love which flow to me from everywhere.
- I am so grateful for supportive friends and a loving family.
- I appreciate and have gratitude for each and every aspect of life which makes me learn and grow.
- I appreciate the persons in my life who always help me in my need.
- I appreciate everything I have in my life and always keep the door open for more blessings.
- The universe supports me and all my desires.
- I am the co-creator of my reality.
- I love nature, birds, animals and plants. They give me the energy to survive and I am grateful to them.
- I see the beauty in nature that surrounds me.

- I see animals as sacred beings and appreciate the gifts they give.
- I give my thanks for the helpful spirits and ancestors who guide me in this journey called life.
- I am blessed.
- I express my gratitude to all.

"Through repetition of thoughts, any idea can be placed in the subconscious mind."

12

Ho'oponopono Technique

A powerful Hawaiian prayer
SITH (Self-Identity Through Ho'oponopono)

Have you heard of Ho'oponopono and the Hawaiian therapist who cured an entire ward of criminally insane patients, without ever meeting any of them or spending a moment in the same room?

The therapist was Dr Ihaleakala Hew Len.

He reviewed each of the patients' files, and then he healed them by healing himself. He cured every patient in the criminally insane ward of Hawaii's State Hospital without ever seeing a single patient.

Dr Len set up an office within the hospital to review his patients' files. While he looked at those files, he would work on himself, and over four years, all the patients were healed. In addition, the staff who had been calling in sick or quit, eventually loved coming to work.

He used the legendary Hawaiian healing and cleansing method Ho'oponopono to accomplish all of this. It is based on healing through loving and taking care of oneself. The amazing results seem like a miracle, but then miracles do happen when you use this method called Self Identity Through Ho'oponopono (SITH).

Dr Len repeated the words "Please forgive me", "I love you", "Thank you" and "I am sorry" over and over again while reviewing each file individually. After a few months, the patients who were shackled were allowed to walk freely, patients were taken off medications, and even the hopeless cases were eventually released back into society.

Dr Joe Vitale, the bestselling author and personal development guru, caught wind of Dr Len's story and wanted to know about this. According to his YouTube video, he mailed Dr Len for a weight loss remedy and he got a reply about a blue solar bottle technique. Then, he decided he had to learn from him. He learned that by using this potent forgiveness and releasing process, one is able to "Clear your mind of subconscious blocks so that destiny and desire can take over and help you get what you truly want from life. It clears out unconsciously accepted beliefs, thoughts, and memories that you don't even know are holding you back." Their collaboration eventually led to the co-authored book *Zero Limits*.

> *"No one wanted the job I did with the criminally insane. They were averaging about one psychologist a month. But I got asked. We had about 25-30 people. Half of them would be in shackles at the ankles or the wrists because*

they were dangerous. They could either kick you or slam you. Everyone would walk with their back to the wall so that they wouldn't get struck. They had no family visits. No one could leave the building. A year-and-a-half later, there was none of that. There were people going out on bus rides, nobody in shackles. The level of medication dropped, and what did I do? I worked on myself. I took 100% responsibility."

–Dr Hew Len

What is Ho'oponopono?

On the surface level, many people have understood Ho'oponopono to be a mantra where one repeats the words 'I'm sorry, please forgive me, thank you, I love you' as a form of mental and spiritual cleaning that could be compared to Buddhist techniques for clearing karma.

The basis of the mantra came from one principle that the Hawaiians teach: *Hurt no one.* Along with this principle, the mantra was used as a form of resolving conflict instead of the arguments continuing to increase. It was believed that the resonance of these four words created harmony and balance. It allowed the conflict you were currently facing to be released and the energy to change when there were surrounding issues.

It has been defined as forgiveness and reconciliation practice, cleansing of 'errors of thought'. The prayer demands that there is a state of peace and resolution, even if there is no ability to let go of the situation. You have to connect to the void, the zero, or you can say, to the universe. The words are able to develop a state of healing that takes place internally, allowing you to accept what is and to move into a more powerful state of mind. This way, you can learn to let go and let love back in.

Forgiveness plays an important part in the whole process, to get rid of any heaviness of guilt in the subconscious. For people living in Hawaii today, Ho'oponopono is less about being a personal shamanic practice through chanting a mantra internally or externally, and more about a traditional system of dispute resolution. It's a practice that still holds the values of making things right and correcting errors. However, in this incarnation, it is focused on making things right with our relations; coming back into the right relationship by correcting errors with living relatives, ancestors and deities as past life regressions help to rectify and clear the past life hurts and karmas. This technique helps to clear blockages which create restrictions to manifestations.

Not only are you resolving conflict with others, you are also resolving the same conflict within yourself. The Ho'oponopono prayer for healing is designed to release those uncertainties that are holding you back from your true potential.

Everything you see, everything you hear, every person you meet, you experience in your mind. You only think it's "out there" and you think that absolves you of responsibility. In fact, it's quite the opposite: you are responsible for everything you think, and everything that comes to your attention. If you saw a WhatsApp post regarding some murder or negative influence, everything you see on your messages is your responsibility. That sounds harsh, but it means that you are also able to clear it, clean it, and through forgiveness change it.

Like many spiritual practices, such as meditation, it's not the practice you do while you're in the crisis, it's the practice you do on a regular basis between the crises that makes it effective when the storm hits.

> *"The truth is, unless you let go, unless you forgive yourself, unless you forgive the situation, unless you realize that the situation is over, you cannot move forward."*

There are four simple steps to this method and the order is not that important. Repentance, forgiveness, gratitude and love are the only forces at work – but these forces have amazing power.

The best part of the updated version of Ho'oponopono is you can do it yourself; you don't need anyone else to be there, you don't need anyone to hear you.

Step 1: Repentance (I AM SORRY)

As I mention above, you are responsible for everything in your mind, even if it seems to be "out there". Once you realize that, it's very natural to feel sorry.

I met with an accident last week. Why was I responsible? Because some days back, I just thought that I was not getting enough time to finalize my book and if I got bed rest from the doctor, then I would be able to complete it. I'm so sorry that someone I know has a broken bone or got injured because of such a thought.

This realization can be painful, and you will likely resist accepting. But when you start noticing your minute thoughts, you will able to catch up with these things.

Like if you are overweight, you may abuse your body by eating inappropriately, or by not doing proper exercises. In fact, people's pains are also caused by abusing your body, as we take more work from it beyond its limits. So, choose something that you already know you've caused for yourself.

"I realize that I abuse my body and take more work from it. I am sorry that I didn't eat appropriate food. I am responsible so I am sorry, I am sorry."

Step 2: Ask for Forgiveness (PLEASE FORGIVE ME}

When you think of your body and the abuse that you have done, feel sorry and ask for forgiveness.

All the sayings and conversations are with the body in case of any disease. But our conversation with the void, universe and the almighty will increase healing the disputed area. Just ask! Please forgive me.

Say it over and over. Mean it.

Remember your remorse from step 1 as you ask to be forgiven.

Step 3: Gratitude (THANK YOU)

Say "THANK YOU" to your body and also to the universe for everything. It doesn't really matter who or what you're thanking. Thank your body for all it does for you. *Thank you* is a magical word, which creates miracles. Thank yourself for being the best you can be. Thank god. Thank the universe. Thank whatever it was that just forgave you.

Just keep saying thank you.

Step 4: Love (I LOVE YOU)

Say it to your body, say it to the universe. Say 'I love you' to the air you breathe, to the plants, to the animals, to the house that shelters you. Say 'I love you' to your problems. Say it over and over, mean it and feel it.

There is nothing as powerful as love.

Dr Hew Len says:

> *"The only purpose in your life and mine is the restoration of our identity, our mind, back to its original state of void or zero (Buddha), of purity of heart (Jesus) and of blank (Shakespeare) through nonstop cleaning."*

13

Path to Inner Peace and Contentment: A Yogic Perspective

"Yoga and meditation is an inward journey from the self to the self; it's knowing, believing and becoming one."

Yoga is a very ancient art and science which originated in India but we cannot determinate exactly when it started. We estimate that it originated about five thousand years ago. Yoga, which means "to yoke or to join", is a practice to unify the mind, body and spirit. Since then, it has taken on so many forms. Most people, when they hear about yoga for the first time, they automatically think about physical postures. In fact, these postures are called *asanas* and they are only a small portion of yoga. All yoga that we practice today is based on the 196 *sutras* which were told more than two thousand years ago by the Indian sage Patanjali. Some call him the *father of yoga* because he wrote not only on yesterday's mind but also of tomorrows'. He only wrote three sutras which monitor the concept of *asanas.*

Yoga is a way of living and not only performing poses on a mat. The western world has focused on the physical part, mostly because they need it. Sedentary lifestyle is a big challenge, today, to enable to sit comfortably for a long period in order to meditate. People get stiff and agitated from long hours of sitting or standing at one place the whole day. Plus, the hectic lifestyle with the pressure of having to be productive and to perform all the time, increases the agitation of the mind when one is trying to relax. The stress of finding success or feeling accomplished in life makes us carry a lot of tension, physically and mentally. One doesn't know how to relax and be calm. Remember, we are human beings, not human doings.

Doing nothing and sipping on a cup of tea while looking outside for a little while before going for a walk or a bath is not an everyday routine. You do it only during vacations. How many vacations do you have in one year? And even then, during the vacation, most of the time is tiring because one wants to visit and discover beautiful places. This is also a way to feel productive and accomplished even during holidays.

These *asanas* are made to prepare the body to remain still with a calm mind.

This chapter is written to give you some understanding of what life of a yogi is. How to practice yoga, every minute of your life? At some point, we all have a strong desire to understand why we are here on earth and what we can do to be part of the change we want to see. We want to see peace in the world, how to find love we want to give and receive, and how to feel this unity with every living thing. Either you ignore it, or you keep going as the materialistic society tells you to live. Keep searching for happiness from the external world rather than finding it within.

Start looking for something different, something that is deeper and makes sense for you. That is how you can learn about yoga. Sometimes, life doesn't give us a choice and illness surrounds us because we are imbalanced. It should actually be taken as a message, a gift that will give us the opportunity to change our lifestyle and makes us listen to our inner self. Otherwise, we will keep fighting and trying to eliminate symptoms, instead of going at the very root of the imbalance to heal ourselves by eliminating the cause.

Introducing yoga in our life is a way to feel more connected with our inner self, and with others. It is a way of bringing balance and stability in our life. We learn to take more distance from situations that could be qualified as "negative" in our life. Then, it doesn't affect us much. Our mood doesn't fluctuate like it used to and we can find peace and tranquility of the mind. It is necessary to relax the mind in order to relax the body. With this relaxation, *prana*, which is the life energy or our energetic body, can flow. While this prana is flowing, we don't feel this draining or exhaustion sensation anymore. All our systems start working better. Breathing, circulation, digestion, movement, secretion, elimination and concentration become very effective and we feel stronger. We acquire a sense of lightness and energy to do what we need to in a focused way, because our mind is not disturbed by negative thoughts. When we are focused, we become more efficient, so we have more time for ourselves.

Eight limbs of Yoga:

The eight limbs of yoga, which are also so called *Ashtanga yoga*, have been written by the Indian sage Patanjali. They are known to be as the shield to fight five *kleshas*: ignorance, ego, attachment, aversion and clinging. Being able to identify these habits or *samskaras* of the mind through continual self-questioning and awareness, we reduce the suffering brought by the afflictions of the mind. Although cycles of behaviour govern our life experience, we can choose whether these will be destructive and negative or constructive and positive.

As this book is made to put into practice all the aspects of yoga, let us start with a check in exercise to go within after this small introduction.

Practice:

- First, log off your computer and turn off your phone.
- Sit down on a chair, back straight, and plant your feet firmly on the floor. Roll your shoulder up, back, and down.
- Close your eyes and concentrate on your breath.
- Is it shallow, short, long or deep? No matter how it is, don't change it; just observe how it is, at that moment.
- After feeling your breath, focus lightly on it.
- Notice the mind's activity while breathing. As thoughts come up, allow them to float without judging them or wanting to push them away.
- After observing them for several times, take a nice deep breath in and let it out in a long exhale.
- Return to normal breathing and reflect on your thoughts. How were they: anxious, spinning, foggy, clear, optimistic?

These exercises presented after each part of the eight limbs of yoga are meant to help you to understand at a deeper level. Understanding something theoretically or to experience it, is totally different. By following these suggested practices, you will experience the benefits of introducing all the aspect of yoga in your daily life.

The eight limbs of yoga are:

1. Yama (Abstinence)
2. Niyama (Observance)
3. Asana (Posture)
4. Pranayama (Breath control)
5. Pratyahara (Sense withdrawal)
6. Dharana (Concentration)
7. Dhyana (Meditation)
8. Samadhi (Contemplation, self-realization, enlightenment)

Yama (Abstinence)

Being the first limb of Ashtanga yoga, Yama is like the roots of the tree, because it is the foundation from which all the rest will grow. Patanjali believed that all life has one source, which is why Yama is so important. There are five different behaviour patterns between the individual and the outside world:

1. Ahimsa (non-violence)
2. Satya (truth)
3. Asteya (non-stealing)
4. Bramacharya (sexual control or abstinence)
5. Aparigraha (lack of greed, non-hoarding)

1.1 Ahimsa (Non-violence)

> *"In the presence of one firmly established in non-violence, all hostilities cease."*
>
> –Yoga sutra 2.35

When we have kind thoughts, speech and action towards others, it will automatically stimulate the same kindness in them. However, Ahimsa is not only about lack of violence, but also an active pursuit of positive actions towards others. To consider others with kind-heartedness and friendliness is a way to be a part of the peace we want to see in the world. Imagine everyone having only thoughtful consideration for others. It doesn't mean to agree on everything and to become close friends with everyone, but knowing that the person in front of us also has feelings, just like us. Since we are all connected, what the person is going through will also affect us.

One should be giving, considering and sensitive. Taking time for people, and being interested in their story gives a better understanding. We all come from different backgrounds with different beliefs and experiences. We all have been through things which are not necessarily apparent, but taint one's life. Being open to the story of others helps us to be more compassionate. Showing respect of one's limitation while believing in the infinite potential, is also a way of considering others.

All these behaviours are very important to apply to ourselves as well. How can we love, be sensitive and caring for others if we can't do it for ourselves? If we see others as a threat or if we compare ourselves with others and think that we are better or worse, how can we be kind and friendly? Everyone has their own strength and weakness according to their experience. We should be inspired by others instead of seeing others as a threat. We should acknowledge the good without envying or putting ourselves down, knowing that everyone is different. To be able to practice Ahimsa, we first need to be aware. Without consciousness of our own habits or tendencies, it is practically impossible to apply because we are only reacting then.

Practice:

Give your time.

- Every week, give some of your time to someone.
- It can be as simple as to ask sincerely how they are feeling and take time to listen.
- You can bring a meal for a friend who is sick, give a small neck and shoulder massage to your mom, write a nice message to someone… be creative!

Try to be more aware of every sentiment. It could be as small as saving a bee out of a pool!

1.2 Satya (Truth)

> *"To one established in truthfulness, actions and their results become subservient."*
>
> –Yoga sutra 2.36

Honesty toward others and self is the first requirement. Lying also includes the distortion of truth. Exaggeration, pretending and manipulating others for our own benefit is also a way of not being totally honest. Obviously, it is not always good to say the whole truth because it could hurt someone and we don't want to hurt anyone. In that case, we keep quiet. Introspection is a very good key. We have to be aware of our own thoughts and actions to make decisions about the proper way to approach people without being judgmental. Tact is also very important. Almost everything can be said when we find a good way to say it and when it comes from a pure intention, people can receive the message better. Those things should be said only if it is really necessary for the benefit of the relation or to improve a situation.

Truth can be relative in the way that we all have our own perception of a situation. We also have a tendency to give others intention, which they may not have. When we are not sure, we should ask people what they mean and why they are doing it. For one situation and ten people participating in it, there will be ten different stories according to how it makes them feel and what their perception was. For each of them, it is their "truth". It is right to say that it is "their experience of the situation", but the truth is actually the objective fact of the situation. No subjectivity. We should acknowledge that everyone has their own experience about one situation and honour it.

Knowing that we make mistakes is crucial. If we can't admit that we are mistaken or at least being able to say that we might be wrong and to double check, it means that we are talking with our ego. We have to always keep questioning ourselves. Why would it be so important to be right? And if we are so sure, we should just take time to explain, show or double check the fact. And if we can't, the person won't believe us; we should accept it and be compassionate.

Practice:

Evaluate your interaction with your surrounding

1. Sit quietly, reflecting on how your answers to the following questions might be impacting your current relationships.
2. Do I or my surrounding use manipulation instead of truthful integrity as a means of winning?
3. Did I or anyone around me withhold love or intimacy as a means to manipulate?
4. Am I scared of being judged if I say the truth about my feelings?
5. When I start to make stories in my head about someone's behaviour or their intention, am I aware of it? Can I ask someone directly about their behaviour or intention to know the truth?

1.3 Asteya (non-stealing)

"Non-stealing" expands beyond the physical act of stealing. Mankind's greed and craving for artificial needs are also considered as stealing. The need to steal happens when there is a lack of faith in ourselves to be able to create what we need. The moment we feel a sense of lack in life, desire and greed arise. We begin to look for something that would fulfill the sensation of emptiness. We may even feel like we are the only ones not having what we think we need to fill this empty sensation.

Lack, insecurity, wanting and feeling incomplete essentially all come from a sentiment of missing something. Yoga means "to unite", which would bring you this feeling of wholeness. By practicing each aspect of yoga on and off the mat, we can reach contentment, to feel satisfied with what we have and what we are.

Although the current state of the world can be overwhelming, this must not affect the clarity of our minds. We should not be filled with worry or anxiety or desire for objects and possessions: this will only add to the existing confusion and dissatisfaction in the world.

Being open to wherever life leads us and not wanting something more or different is also a way of practicing Asteya. We have to accept our limitation and live with how it is in the present moment. It is done by dealing with the reality of now, that we can actually grow and improve ourselves. If we only focus on what we don't have and what we are not, we are only going to lose our energy. Instead, better to accept the situation and work with it without greed.

Practice:

Gratefulness and body scan

1. Lay down in Shavasana in a quiet place.
2. Close your eyes and feel your respiration for ten breaths.
3. Focus your attention to your feet and say: 'thank you for supporting me; I am very grateful that you are supporting me' all day long.
4. Focus your attention towards your legs and say thank you. I am grateful that I can walk wherever I want.
5. Lead your attention to your hips, lower back and lower belly and say: thank you for protecting all my reproductive organs.
6. Focus your attention to your rib cage and say: thank you for helping the organs in my chest, such as my heart and my lungs to allow me to breathe deeply and bring oxygen for all the cells in my body.

7. Bring your awareness to your arms and hands and say: thank you for authorizing me to cook, drink, write, hug, and take care of myself and others in many ways so freely.
8. Focus your attention towards you head and say: thanks to my mouth for allowing me to taste food. To my nose to smell, to my eyes to see and to my mind to understand and reflect.
9. Then, say thank you for all that you have in your life.
10. Finish with your hands on your heart and focus on your heart chakra while breathing deeply for ten breathes.

1.4 Bramacharya (Abstinence)

"To establish in continence, vigor is gained."

–Yoga sutra 2.38

If we translate it literally, in classical yoga, Bramacharya means abstinence from sexual activity in thought, word and deed. The reason for it is because the seminal fluid is to provide energy and stamina to the brain and nerves, and to build up prana. However, modern interpretations have a more open view of Bramacharya which would be to have moderation in all things. The common misconception is mostly about celibacy because it is often considerate irrelevant in modern culture, although the right use of energy is more prevalent now than ever. Abstinence is also referred as "behaviour which leads to Brahman". Brahman is considered as the creator in Hinduism and Yogic terminology, so what we want to point is to take action that will guide you to "the divine" or the "higher power".

Regarding Brahmacharya as "right use of energy", it encourages us to be aware of how we use and direct our energy. Of course, it also evokes to direct our energy away from external desires. Those pleasures can seem so satisfying at the moment, but instead of leading us to peace and happiness within, it can actually bring more suffering. Sexuality can easily be another way to try to find peace on the external level. That is why it is recommended to moderate it, so your attention can be diverted to raise consciousness and find peace within.

The aim of moderation is to avoid waste of energy. Gossiping, indulging in fantasy, nostalgia or anticipating future events is to be kept away. Plus, many people have a tendency to push themselves or to be excessive in things that they do. We should acknowledge it and try to have a more moderate approach. We also have to recognize if we are more kind to hold back and remain in comfort. Too much of anything brings problems. Too little may be inadequate.

Right now, there seems to be an over-emphasis on how busy we should be. The more productive and more efficient we are, the better it seems to be from the outside. Filling our schedule can be impressive, but we have to know if it is really worthwhile. Most of the time, it is another story from within. We need to keep time to rest and to include rejuvenating moments in our schedule to find calmness. This is also the way to find balance in the use of our energy.

Practice:

Mindful schedule

1. What is it that really makes us feel good and relaxed? Maybe a bath with some music and candles or a long walk with a

break at your favourite café to have a cup of tea while reading a book, or just to sit on your yoga mat for some breathing exercises.

2. Whatever it might be, we should make sure that we take time for ourselves and put in your schedule a place or free time. It should be as precious as a meeting you have or an appointment to the doctor.

1.5 Aparigraha (Lack of greed, non-attachment)

> *"When non-greed is confirmed, a thorough illumination of the how and why of one's birth comes."*
>
> –Yoga sutra 2.39

> *"Let your concern be with the action alone, and never with the fruit of action. Do not let the results of your action to be your motive, and do not be attached to inaction."*
>
> –Krishna

Aparigraha is an attitude that should be applied to material possessions, relationships and nature. *"We came into this world without anything, and we will leave it without taking anything with us."* Therefore, no matter how many things we acquire, they never truly belong to us. In fact, too many possessions bring distraction into the mind. A life of simplicity is conducive to owning only what is necessary. One should think of getting rid of everything that hasn't been used within the last year. Not necessary to be excessive either, memories are good to keep to a certain extent. Yet, if we hoard every single thing in our life, we could ask ourselves: What are we holding on to? Especially, if we keep them where we don't ever see them again.

Non-greed is also not to focus on the result of what we are doing. It is more about the journey than the destination. How often we worry about how a project will end up, how our meal will taste while we are cooking it, or where a relationship will lead to, that we can't be in the moment and really enjoy what is happening now? If we don't put all our attention on success or on our expectation, we can make the best out of what is happening in the present moment.

Change is the only thing that we can expect. It is the law of nature – nothing is static. Even if it seems like our days are similar in our daily routine, in reality, it is not the same. Our emotions are constantly changing, our body is also changing every minute, with cells regenerating, blood flowing, bones wearing down and then being stimulated to build up again. Becoming attached to a state of mind, like the sensation of joy, happiness or our appearance, our possession is a ticket for sufferance. It would also be a resistance to live life fully. Obviously, we would like to remain joyful all the time, but reality is that pain and sadness is also a part of life. Knowing that everything is in a state of constant change, we can welcome it and experience it totally while knowing that this will also pass.

Aparigraha is also about generosity and giving. With learning how to give, we learn how to receive. Most of the time, people are more comfortable to give than to receive. We should understand that when we give, there must be a receiver. And when we give, we like the receiver to be happy with it and to welcome it. That means we should give this pleasure to others and be grateful when something is offered to us. Giving and receiving are different aspects of the flow of energy in the universe.

Practice

Detach from your possessions

- Every time we buy something, we should check if there is something we don't use anymore, that we could get rid of by giving it to someone, or throwing it, if it is not good anymore.
- Every change of weather, we should clean our closet and give some clothes away to friends, family or a place where they can give them to people in need.

Observing ourselves

- Let us observe our reaction when change occurs.
- Are we agitated, scared, stressed, sad, or nostalgic?
- Let us not judge it, just be aware of it. This will allow having more distance from it and not identifying ourselves with our emotions while allowing them to exist. Then, relax and let things be how they are and let them go when it goes.

Niyama

The Niyamas refer to duties towards ourselves, or inner observances. They are intended to help us build character. When we work with the Niyamas, we're guided from the grossest aspects of ourselves to the truth deep within.

1. Shauch (cleanliness)
2. Santosha (contentment)

3. Tapas (discipline, austerity)
4. Svadhyaya (self-inquiry)
5. Ishvara Pranidhana (surrender to god)

2.1 Shauch (Cleanliness)

Shauch is cleanliness on every level of being: physical, mental and emotional. To keep a clean environment, is very important to also be clean in our mental and emotional state. When we live in a place where everything is upside down, our mind cannot concentrate and focus because there is no order around. Maybe some of us have experienced a situation where we need to concentrate, like studying or doing our tax, and getting irritated because we can't find the papers we need and every step takes much longer. At the end, we are exhausted and frustrated and then we feel like we need to compensate with something that would sooth us – like a bag of chips or a chocolate bar. What if everything had been in order and we knew exactly where and how to find what we needed, getting it done efficiently? Then, creating the space to do something else is more relaxing, like going for a meditation or lying down with soothing music, or even cooking a nice meal.

Practice:

- Every day, chose a space where you will clean your environment.
- That place can be your desktop at work, your closet, your bag/purse, doing laundry, etc.
- We should also take time for our hygienic health. Cut your nails when you need, brush your hair, shave, use cream if

you need too. Feel like you're worthy of caring for yourself.

- To remain "clean" emotionally, we have to make sure we don't stop our emotions from coming out. Allow yourself to cry, to get angry or to laugh, if you need. This doesn't mean to explode with a strong reaction, but to take time to recognize our emotions and meditate on the sensations in our body and then be able to take right action about it.
- Talk to someone you have confidence in, who can listen to you properly without advise or judgment, that can cause further confusion.
- Drawing, writing or singing are also ways to express our emotions.

2.2 Santosha (Contentment)

One should live with only what is necessary. If we don't have self-satisfaction, we remain in an agitated and frustrated state. Being satisfied is not only about what we have, but also about what we are. If we think that we would be happy only if we had a different appearance or with a bigger place or a better partner, we can't find peace. Acceptance leads to contentment. Feeling happy with what we are and what we have at the moment is not easy to achieve, but it is the only way to find calmness.

Sending love to ourselves when we look into the mirror and gazing into our own eyes while sending compassion to our soul is a good way to find love within. When we are in our house, at work or out with friends, we should take time to acknowledge what we have and be grateful for it.

It doesn't mean that we can't do anything to improve the situation we are in. Essentially, it is a way to be content at every moment of our life, while not having expectation or constant desire for something different. Ambition is a good thing when it is started with a good intention, like to help others or to take care of the environment.

Practice:

- At the end of every day, let us make a list of ten things we are grateful for.
- The list should have at least one thing that shows how we are happy with ourselves, with someone else, with a situation and something that we have. It can be as simple and deep as: I am grateful to have two legs to walk on. Sometimes, we don't realize how lucky we are until we lose it.

2.3 Tapas (Discipline)

The word *Tapas* comes from the root Sanskrit verb "*tap*" which means "to burn", and recalls a sense of "fiery discipline" or "passion". In this sense, it can mean to pursue self-discipline, a passion and courage in order to burn "impurities" physically, mentally and emotionally. Discipline is not about being hard on ourselves; it is more about this fiery passion that helps us to get up in the morning to go for a run or for yoga practice. Taking the decision not to drink too much, not too eat too much or getting up earlier to have time to meditate or to read something that will help us for our day is also a way to introduce tapas. These actions remove "impurities" of the mind. Impurities are the negative thoughts that drive us, like "you're not good enough" or "you're too weak".

The element of fire is also the element of transformation. When we apply Tapas in our life, it means that we will try different things; we will have determination to apply what is really important to us by not letting fear or our ego getting in the way. Tapas is a way of acting from love and positivity.

Practice:

Develop an evening routine

A regular routine in the evening can be very helpful in finding peace and tranquility after a long and hectic day. It would allow us to release stress and to fall asleep more rapidly.

- Eating at a regular time allows us to have a proper digestion before going to bed. Around 6 to 7 is usually a good time to have dinner.
- Around 8:30 p.m., we can do something calm and soothing with our friends, family or on our own. It could be a small walk, listening to music, drawing, reading, a bath, meditation, etc.
- Having a warm drink such as some herbal tea or milk with turmeric, cardamom and cinnamon to relax.
- Going to bed around ten and allowing time for a self-massage on our temples, forehead, shoulders, neck and feet with essential oils like lavender or eucalyptus and then, washing our hands with soap.
- Lying down on our back and putting one hand on our belly and one on our chest to practice abdominal breathing. Each time we inhale, feeling that our body is taking all the love, the energy and peace from the universe, and each time we exhale, feeling that our body gets more and more relaxed while releasing tension. We should do it until we fall asleep, or for at least ten minutes.

- One should try to get around eight hours of sleep every night (maybe a bit less or more according to the need of your body to function at its best).

2.4 Svadhyaya (Self-inquiry)

Svadhyaya essentially means self-study: knowledge of the self and scripture study. To study the scripture about good guidelines for spirituality like *The Yoga Sutras of Patanjali, The Bhaghavad Gita,* and *The Hatha Yoga Pradipika* helps to give an understanding and aim for the rational mind. Reading an inspiring book helps to create space for different thinking. We have been through so much since our childhood at school, with our parents and our surroundings, but we did not necessarily have the chance to have some education on spirituality. Although it is good to read about it, it is necessary to reflect upon it and see how it resonates with us, and how to really apply it in our daily life.

Self-study is to observe ourselves, to have a continuous awareness to be able to understand our own personal shortcomings. Being conscious of ourselves literally means to observe our thoughts, the way we talk to others, the way we hold ourselves while walking or standing. Practicing Svadhyaya includes Satya (honesty), Tapas (discipline) and Ahimsa (non-violence). It is very important that while observing ourselves, we do it from an honest standpoint, which also takes discipline, because it is not always comfortable to see the truth within us. Furthermore, it is crucial to remain non-judgmental and non-critical towards ourselves.

Practice:

Look back on your day.

- What did I do right after I woke up this morning?
- How was I feeling when I woke up this morning?
- Was I rushing around this morning, running late, or wondering how I'd be able to squeeze everything into the day?
- Did I make time to eat? What did I eat? How did I feel eating it?
- Did I find time for myself, to take a pause, breathe or laugh?
- What were the negative thoughts toward me or a situation or someone else?
- What were the positive thoughts I had for me or a situation or someone else?
- How am I feeling right now?

2.5 Ishvara Pranidhana (surrender to god)

First of all, the word "god" is a very tricky one since there are many conceptions of it and some even have a total aversion to it. While yoga is not about religion or does not force any concept of god, it still implies that something bigger than us exists, something more profound and pure. According to Satchidananda, Isvara Pranidhana means to offer our action up to "the divine" and humanity, because we are all connected through consciousness. In this sense, god is not a particular character; it represents this collective consciousness and therefore represents all of us too.

Surrendering to god is a way of letting go. Easier to say than to do! Often, we feel like we can control everything in our life and we feel responsible for it. Of course, we have the power of creating our own reality, but aren't there so many situations where you wish you could change it, but feel powerless? Letting go and understanding that we don't have the power on everything? For some people it can sound really scary, not having control, but looking at it from a different perspective, it takes some pressure off our shoulders.

For example, if we leave for work one morning and we go through the same routine, and then, something happens. It could be that you are stuck in traffic because there is an accident that morning, or your daughter is sick and you have to stay home even if you had an important meeting. Whatever it is, we could either get super stressed out and concerned and then have a really bad time, or we can surrender to it and see how "life" or "god" had another plan for us at that time. Why should we take all the responsibilities? When we can surrender to uncomfortable situations in our life instead of always reacting to it, we can find so much more peace and rest. Not always feeling that we have to do something about it, just surrender.

Practice:

Direct love

- Calm yourself and clear your mind. Concentrate on deep, regular breaths.
- Concentrate now on your heart chakra and visualize a white light coming in while inhaling, and the light going out while exhaling.
- Now direct this light and love in four ways:
  – May all beings be free from danger; may all be safe.

- May all beings be happy; may all have peace.
- May all beings have physical well-being; may all be healthy.
- May all beings have ease of well-being; may all be free from suffering.

- Then, direct these feelings towards yourself and let them wash over you and fill you.
- Now, visualize a person or a situation that is more difficult to accept, in which you may experience anger, aversion or sadness, and direct love to it.

Asana

> *"Prior to everything, asana is spoken of as the first part of Hatha Yoga. Having done asana, one attains steadiness of body and mind, freedom from disease and lightness of the limbs."*

1:17 Hatha Yoga Pradipika

The actual meaning of *yogasana* is a "position which is comfortable and steady". In this context, asanas are practiced to develop the ability to sit comfortably in one position for an extended period of time, which is necessary for meditation. The hatha yogis found that certain specific body position allows opening the energy channels and psychic centers. By controlling our body through this practice, it enables us to control the mind and energy. Actually, it is a tool to higher awareness.

Firstly, we need an empty and quiet space to practice. A nonslip mat, a strap or belt, firm cotton or wool blankets, wooden or foam block and maybe a metal or wooden chair – these props help us to keep a good alignment during our practice to avoid injuries. We also need a strong awareness, non-violence towards ourselves since yoga is not about getting deeper in the pose, but about observing ourselves, our greed, and our limitation and not reacting to it.

There are many kinds of yoga (Hatha, Ashtanga, Iyengar, Vinyasa flow, Kundalini, Yin, Restorative, etc.), so it can be good to try a few to see what suits us the best according to our nature. Then, stick to it and practice! By sticking to a certain style, one can go deeper in the practice, although sometimes we can see how we feel that day and practice according to our need, which is also a way of listening to our body. If we feel like an ashtanga practice is too much, maybe what we need is more a restorative or a yin class at that time.

It is recommended to have a teacher at first to guide us and correct us so we don't get injured. When we feel more confident, it is good to start a self-practice as well as attending yoga classes for a different challenge.

Practice:

Tadasana is a good way to start the physical practice. Observe our standing habits. Where is our weight on our feet? How is our pelvis tilted? Are we hanging on our lower back? How are our shoulders and our neck? What about our mind? Is it agitated? Calm?

Finding steadiness of the mind and body in our mountain pose (tadasana) before we start our practice and setting an intention. It could be something as simple as being present or dedicating our energy to someone or something.

Sun salutation

- Stand with feet hip-width apart and parallel. Distribute the weight evenly on the mounds of each toe and your heel. Spread your toes on the ground and feel the energy lifting upward, allowing the spine to lengthen and open the shoulders. Breathe through your abdomen gently.

Tadasana

- Inhale while lifting your arms up, pointing your fingertips toward the sky, gazing at your thumbs.

Urdhva Hastasana

- Exhale while you hinge forward from your hip joint and bring your palms towards your feet.

Uttanasana

- Inhale and straighten your back while putting your hands on your shin.

Urdhva Uttanasana

- Exhale while putting both hands on the ground and bend your knees to step into plank pose. Breathe. Then, lower to the earth.

Chaturanga Dandasana

- Inhale and push your hands under your shoulders to bring your upper body up. Make sure your shoulders are open.

Urdhva Mukha Svanasana (your legs are off the floor) or Bhujangasana (thighs remain on the floor)

- Exhale, tuck your toes under, push into the mounds of your hand and use the strength of your core to lift your hips up and back. Establish a straight line from your wrists, shoulders, spine and hips, making a "V" shape. You can slightly bend your knees to allow elongation of the spine.

Ado Mukha Svanasana

- Inhale while stepping both legs in between your hands and put your hands on your shin while stretching your spine forward.

Urdhva Uttanasana

- Exhale and fold forward completely, softening your back.

Uttanasana

- Inhale and rise fully and radiantly with a straight spine and your hands towards the sky and look up.

Urdhva Hastasana

- Exhale and bring your hands in prayer pose while feeling the heart-opening effects of this sequence.

Pranayama

> *"Pranayama is the regulation of the oncoming and outgoing flow of the breath with retention."*
>
> –Yoga sutra, 2.49

Prana is the vital force. The word pranayama is a combination of the Sanskrit words *prana* and *ayama*. Prana is the principle of life or aliveness. Ayama means expansion or the extension of the range of prana. Breath is closely linked with prana and before extending this vital force, we need to control it, which is known as Prana Nigraha.

The breath is the most vital process of our body. By practicing pranayama, we improve this vital energy, which can take the practitioner to a higher level of consciousness. The breath is intimately connected to the mind, so if we have an agitated breath, our mind is also agitated. Furthermore, improving the respiratory efficiency allows a tremendous relief to the vital organs. Before any kind of breath practice, one should know what the correct way of breathing is.

Practice

First of all, lie down in Shavasana or sit in a comfortable position and observe the nature of your breathing pattern while visualizing your respiratory system. Put one hand on your belly and one hand on your chest to really understand your way of breathing.

Inhale

Your diaphragm goes down as the air enters into your lungs. This action of your diaphragm widens your rib cage and pushes your abdomen downward and forward. That is where the inhalation should start.

For a full inhalation, your upper lungs will get filled with air by the contraction of intercostal muscles, but the diaphragm remains the main muscle for breathing.

Exhale

Your diaphragm returns to its original position, and air is expelled from your lungs. Your abdomen draws in and up when you breathe out. Exhalation is passive.

You can exaggerate it at first to really feel the abdominal breathing.

Most people don't use their diaphragm properly and only use their chest to breathe. This is very stressful for all the area of the shoulders and neck. Also, many people do the opposite action – while inhaling, they push the belly which doesn't allow the expansion of the diaphragm and encourages those higher muscle to work more. And then, while exhaling, they swell the belly. This reverse breathing can create chronic tension in the neck and shoulders and can bring irregular biological rhythms – menstrual flow, constipation, frequent or uneven urination, insomnia, elevated blood pressure and even tachycardia.

When we go back to a normal way of breathing, some of the most obvious symptoms of stress start to decrease and can even cease. Focusing on our breathing has a sedative effect, if done for two to ten minutes. It will lower our blood pressure and respiratory rate. It can also be a very good tool to help us to fall asleep more rapidly. This needs a strong awareness of the breath. We should observe it when we go through strong emotions and during our yoga practice.

Secondly, different pranayama techniques can be practiced. Most of them are practiced sitting cross-legged. The best time to practice is early morning on an empty stomach. It is also important to know which pranayama is appropriate to our condition, as some should not be practiced during menstruation, pregnancy or if we have digestive problems, because they involve abdominal contraction and an upward motion. Fast rhythms or breath retention should not be practiced if one has asthma, hypertension, heart disease or during pregnancy. This is not the full list of precautions, so it is always better to check with a health professional or yoga therapist first.

Some of the pranayamas are energizing and detoxifying – like kapalabhati (skull shining breath) with a fast and strong contraction of the abdomen to exhale, or bhastrika (bellows breath) with forceful exhalation and forceful inhalation.

Others are balancing and relaxing, such as nadi shodhana (alternate nostril breathing) or sama vritti (equal breathing) when inhalation and exhalation are equal length. Bhramari (humming bee) is also a tranquilizing pranayama.

Pranayama technique should be taught by a professional before applying them in your life.

Pratyahara

> *"One who is able to withdraw their senses from sensory object, such as the tortoise that draws its limbs within the shell, is firmly fixed in perfect consciousness."*
>
> –*Gita* 2.58

When awareness arises, we can see how the mind is filled with events of the external world. Our mind constantly goes back in the past or gets lost imagining stories about the future. Our mind gets distracted very easily by our different senses, such as eyes (form), ears (sounds), nose (smell), etc. As a result, the mind is always agitated and distracted. We need to work on these modifications of the mind to prepare for meditation. To be able to do this, we need to control our senses. That is Pratyahara: dissociating the mind from sensory objects.

It begins with objective awareness. We have to practice by looking at a situation from a distance, without being affected by it. Then only the mind can slowly start withdrawing itself from the situation. This can also induce a deep state of relaxation, peace of mind and strong concentration.

According to Patanjali, if we establish Pratyahara, we can move forward towards the next stages: the practice of Dharana (concentration) and thereafter Dhyana (meditation), which ultimately results in Samadhi (self-realization).

Practice:

- Whenever we feel hungry because of a good aroma, a nice looking dish or a rumbling in our stomach, we should start to observe the thoughts and sensations in our body.
- See if there is any clinging or aversion toward the situation.
- Let's be more curious about the sensation in our body. It could be that we have more saliva in our mouth or we feel a sensation of emptiness in our stomach.
- Whatever it is, let's just keep on observing and be aware of the thoughts coming.
- We may realize that the more we are attached to these sensations and thoughts, the more we are agitated.
- Reflect on the power of the mind.

Dharana (concentration) and Dhyana (meditation)

> *"Concentration is binding the mind to one place."*
>
> –Yoga sutra, 3.1

Dharana is the ability to hold the mind on one object of meditation. The object can be a mantra, a symbol, the breath, or anything one chooses. This effort is made to direct the mind inward to a deep state of awareness. Regular practice is very important as it allows the mind to return quicker to the object of meditation when one gets lost in its thoughts. The ultimate goal is to experience the highest state of consciousness. However, we cannot deny the other benefits that it induces, like the ability to face difficult situations in life and the ability to maintain inner joy. When Dharana becomes continuous so that there is no discontinuity in the concentration, we are in Dhyana.

Practice:

Meditation

- Find a calm room and make sure you are in comfortable clothes. Early morning before breakfast or at night, before going to bed, is a good time for meditation.
- Sit in lotus or half lotus position on the floor, on a cushion, so your hips are higher than your knees. If this is not comfortable for you, find a position that suits you.
- Keep your hands on your knees or palms together in the center and close your eyes. Make sure your back is straight and your chin is parallel to the floor, or slightly tucked in.

- Start to focus on your breath. Feel the air going in through your nostrils while inhaling and out while exhaling.
- Each time you find yourself lost in your thoughts, just bring your attention back to your breath and the sensations around and in your nostrils.
- Make sure you don't judge your thoughts, be equanimous. Be gentle and compassionate as you bring back your attention.
- Thoughts are like clouds in your inner sky. You can be aware of them, but don't try to catch any, let them pass.

Samadhi (Self-realization, enlightenment)

When Dhyana is continuous for a long time, it becomes Samadhi. This is the state of deep concentration which allows us to stay aware continuously. The reason why we refer to self-realization is because it is not about escapism, floating away or being extremely joyful; it's about realizing the very life within us right now at this very moment.

Samadhi is also a state where there is no separation. We stop identifying with 'I' which we often used to describe with what we like, what we have done, what we want or our role. Most of the time, there is something we would like to change about it, to improve or to get rid of. We can ask ourselves: who is doing the seeking? Who are we if everything we describe ourselves with is actually impermanent?

Samadhi is encouraging to let go of these stories, cease seeking and see the reality as it is, "equally", without disturbance of the mind. The thoughts, the emotions, likes, dislikes, pleasure or habits are looked at with equanimity, so we can see the reality of what it is without being disturbed by the fluctuation of the mind. Only then can we detach from 'I' and start to feel like we are all part of this universal consciousness and no longer feel separated from others and our environment. It is a state of constant awareness of the whole.

A calm mind is the most powerful thing in the universe. As it creates joy and happiness.

If you are able to silence the mind when its services are not required, at least for some seconds, then it will create the path to peace and contentment. A person who can silence the inner chatter of his mind is free from worries, anxieties, fears and any type of tensions.

True control of the mind is not just the ability to concentrate on one thought (positive) and disregard other thoughts (negative). It is the ability to cleanse the mind completely and make it silent. Try the technique to silence your mind. Firstly, try to silence your mind as you will not think about anything for ten seconds and after that, practice the same for fifteen seconds... and more...The time will come when you will be able to control the thoughts, whether they are positive or negative. Then you will be the master of your mind and thoughts. This silence brings peace, contentment, happiness and bliss. This silence is not the silence of sleep. It is the silence of power, happiness, love and enhanced awareness. It is the silence of the subconscious mind.

How to attain inner peace and contentment?

A positive mental attitude towards inner peace and contentment is very necessary.

Meditation

The calmness of the soul and spirit: If you do not meditate yet, you are missing out on a very important process which can change your life. Meditating has an enormous impact in all the areas of your life. Meditation is a process in which your soul is directly connected to the almighty universe and can converse with the universe. If you have a lot on your mind and you feel like your thoughts are driving you crazy, meditation can help you find peace, cleanse your brain and give you calmness. Simply close everything, sit back, close your eyes, and clear your mind of every single thought. Focus on the emptiness. Focus on the formless almighty, the universe. You will be surprised what a mere ten minutes of meditation can do to turn things around for you.

Love to look at nature

We spend so much time confined in buildings of iron and concrete and bricks that we quickly forget where we come from. It is natural for us to feel so good, pleasant, calm and peaceful when you take a walk in a park barefoot to connect with the earth or cycling on a trail in the forest. Watching the stillness of a tree, with the wind blowing through its branches calmly, watching colourful butterflies, the birds, the flowers, how the different colours and shapes have been created by the almighty, it is a sight that not only inspires, but that can find peace within it. If you feel overwhelmed, take a stroll outside where there are tons of trees and far from the city. Be there and just enjoy the sights, the sounds, and the peace.

Smiling, the best medicine

Whenever you are laughing or smiling, something interesting happens. Not only does something happen on a chemical level to make you feel better and light, but it also helps to relieve all stress and negativity from entering your body. A simple smile can make such a difference.

Everyone in my family was worried and tensed about my accident. In fact, my husband was like he would weep at that time. As I woke up from sedations, I smiled and said, "It is okay...It happens in life. I will take rest as I was so starved of sleeping" and everyone started smiling.

After that, the environment of the room of the hospital became positive and calm. So, whenever you find yourself in a similar predicament, just think of the silver lining, and don't be shy to poke fun at yourself. I always make fun of me to make myself and everyone happy. You will quickly realize that peace finds its way much more easily to you when you smile.

Care for all and serve humanity

You will never find peace by being self-consumed and only worrying about your own needs and wants. When you begin to genuinely care about other people, so much goodness comes right out. Care is all about the strength of unconditional love. This only helps to strengthen your inner peace. It can be people close to you, or pure strangers, but any act of kindness, smile or prayer will ease your way towards peace. When you help other people, you will stop focusing on your so-called problems as your mind becomes busy.You will realize that your life isn't so bad after seeing more miserable and poor people in life. You feel very calm and peaceful when you serve others without any motive.

When I join "Cleanliness Drive on Railway stations and other public places" every month, I felt like I was serving humanity selflessly, and that was a heaven on earth. My entire being had changed, all the stress vanished and feelings of overwhelming joy overshadowed me".

There is great peace and wisdom in thinking and caring about other people, and for humanity.

Hope for the best

Hope is something you can never afford to lose. With hope you always have a path towards peace and to fulfilling desires.

I personally never lose hope. Whatever delay my work takes, I stay in good faith and be calm and also try my best to give the proper desirable results. Whenever you get too stressed out and overwhelmed by your own life, you forget that hope. Remember the sun always shines after a rainy day. When I lost the sensation in my half right hand, it was like doctors had lost the hope and said; "Nerves will never be recovered if they are damaged and it will be tough for you to write with your hand." I didn't lose hope, at that time I was writing this book in my dairy, but after that, I started typing it on the laptop and practiced from my left hand to complete this book. It meant I didn't lose hope and I was about to finish my book.

I find immense peace in just knowing, deep within my heart, that everything will be ok. With hope, I know that whatever seems terrible is only temporary and that soon enough, things will be just fine. This lifts off all of that negativity from my entire being, and I feel better pretty much instantly.

Live your life fully

> *"Never continue in a job you don't enjoy. If you're happy in what you're doing, you'll like yourself, you'll have inner peace. And if you have that, along with physical health, you'll have more success than you could possibly have imagined."*
>
> –Roger Caras

When you do what you enjoy and have passion, there is a natural peace that arises within. You are in alignment with the universe. This also leads to a lot more success than if you are stuck on the unsatisfied work.

To enjoy life, you have to love each and every moment of your life and see miracles in each and every aspect of life.

Be careful with your inner peace.

"Never be in a hurry; do everything quietly and in a calm spirit. Do not lose your inner peace for anything whatsoever, even if your whole world seems upset and even if you are going to lose everything, everything is in divine timing."

Your inner peace is most important in the whole process. If you are getting disturbed with any circumstances and events, then you are spoiling your vibrational frequency. Stepping out of the positivity, you will never attain the peace. You have to live "sehaj" and "saral". You have to live with the flow, whatever is going on.

People don't get the difference between contentment and happiness.

Why choose contentment over happiness? A couple of important reasons:

Happiness can go up or down each moment, but contentment is a more stable state of mind and soul.

We tend to seek to increase happiness by adding things like eating good food, excitement for a party, full body massage followed by a warm bath, time with a loved one and enjoyment with kids, go for a wonderful movie, but contentment is a skill that allows you to subtract things and still be content and happy with whatever there is. It's the whole spiritual mental satisfaction.

Contentment is about being happy with who you are and whatever you have. It's the game of satisfaction of whatever you have and still have the full feeling of gratitude in your subconscious mind.

After my accident, I just tried to stand and then I saw that half of my right hand was not with me. I thought it might have been cut down and then I sat on the road and started praying and said "thank you" to almighty as it's you who gave me this body, whatever you want you can take and thank you for the whole body, which was safe.

Suddenly, people came and picked up my half hand from my backside which was hanging over due to the whole breakage of the elbow and I was not able to see that. Now what I learned in the whole process was that when you are regularly trying to make your vibrations high and being in the positive state of mind, you come into the stage of contentment and go with a flow. The flow of immense trust, satisfaction and surrendering to the formless almighty.

And while many might say, "*Sure, you can say that now that you've reached a certain level of success,*" I think that's wrong. Many people who achieve success don't find contentment, and are always driven to want more, and are unhappy with themselves. Many people who are poor or don't have a "successful" career have also found contentment and are satisfied with their lives.

Contentment has actually driven any success that you have found. It helped to get out of debt, it helped to change habits, and it has made me a better wife, mother, friend, and colleague, perhaps even a better author.

The path to contentment is to free your heart and soul from any type of negativity and self-demoralization. The path of contentment is to realize yourself. It's to realize the true nature of the creator and always feel the presence of it all around you.

Let go of all the pains, hurts, and guilt from yourself and free yourself from all the negativity.

People think that they will be merged in the super soul and attain completion of life when they die. But your body is not an obstacle for pure contentment. Your thoughts and your vibrations are obstacles in it if it is not appropriated.

When you feel happy and raise the vibration level of happiness state, your soul starts feeling the super soul; it will be the remembrance of the almighty all the time. The feeling of super soul makes you contented when you feel like you are already a part of the super soul and that super soul is protecting you. It is the real heaven, the state of oneness, when all seems to be the part of super soul and all are one. The feeling of heaven is always and always here. It is the stage where your vibration is in the uppermost stage. You feel that your soul merges into the super soul and you are very light.

Here you come in the stage of "oneness", where you feel each and every person is the part of the super soul, is the part of the universe, comes from the same source and you all are one. No difference of basics, only perceptions do differ.

The yogis and saints do meditation to go on an upper vibration frequency to feel the merging of the soul with super soul and can feel anything, can go anywhere without their physical mortal bodies.

Planets, moon, stars... all can be travelled in less than the fraction of seconds. The only bet to get all these things is to be happy and be at the highest frequency, in which time and space do not matter. Only love, gratitude and happiness make it possible.

Be happy! Be Grateful! Be contented!